Teaching About
Native Americans

Karen D. Harvey

Lisa D. Harjo

Jane K. Jackson

National Council for the Social Studies
Bulletin No. 84

ISBN 0-87986-059-6

National Council for the Social Studies

OVER
E
76.6
.H37
1990

Library of Congress Catalog Card Number : 90-61482

ISBN-087986-059-6

Copyright © 1990

by

National Council for the Social Studies

3501 Newark Street N.W.

Washington, D.C. 20016-3167

#21722350

Editorial Staff on this publication: Salvatore J. Natoli and Pamela D. Hollar, NCSS

Layout and design by Dan Kaufman, Coordinator of Desktop Publishing, NCSS

Bear figure on cover by Karen Recktenwald, Littleton, Colorado

105517

TABLE OF CONTENTS

ABOUT THE AUTHORS

Karen D. Harvey is Director of Staff Development for Cherry Creek Schools in Denver, Colorado, and serves as adjunct professor of education at the University of Colorado at Denver. She teaches graduate courses in social studies and multicultural education and has had a long-time interest in Native Americans and in Indian education. Dr. Harvey has been active in the National Council for the Social Studies and the Colorado Council for the Social Studies, and serves as a consultant to Rough Rock School in Chinle, Arizona.

Lisa D. Harjo, Director of the Early Childhood Program, Circle of Learning, at the Denver Indian Center, is an elementary school teacher. Long active in Indian education, Lisa has served in many leadership roles and has written and published *The Circle Never Ends*, an American Indian curriculum model. She is current President of the Colorado Indian Education Association and serves as a member of the American Indian Advisory Council of the Denver Public Schools. Lisa is a member of the Choctaw Nation.

Jane K. Jackson is a social studies teacher at Smoky Hill High School in Denver, Colorado. She has also taught at the junior high school and adult levels. Jane has been involved with anthropological study of Native Americans as well as initiating and participating in cultural exchanges between Navajo and Pueblo schools. She has nurtured a personal interest in Native American spirituality and studied Shamanic healing. Jane was a 1986 nominee for Colorado Teacher of the Year.

ACKNOWLEDGEMENTS

Many friends and family members have been generous with their time, their ideas, and, most importantly, with their friendship and support. They have been our teachers and we would like to thank: Dr. Gary Knight, Professor, Fort Lewis College, Durango, Colorado; Dan Estell, Principal, Rough Rock Elementary School, Rough Rock, Arizona; Ernest Dick, Navajo, President of the School Board, Rough Rock Community School, Rough Rock, Arizona; Dr. Gary Coan, Former Director of Education at Rough Rock School, now at Zuni Pueblo, Zuni, New Mexico; Alfred Yazzie, Director, Navajo Resource Center, Rough Rock, Arizona; Perry Ray Davis, Choctaw; Ione B. Davis; Mody B. Harjo, Seminole/Creek; Tvhonkne Jane Harjo, Seminole/Creek/Choctaw; Sena Koleepkv Harjo, Seminole/Creek/Choctaw; Jan N. Jacobs, Osage, Chair, American Indian Education Advisory Council, Denver Public Schools; Farrell Howell, Pawnee, Principal, Grand Middle School, Denver Public Schools; Debra Echo-Hawk, Pawnee/Otoe, Chairperson, Native American Title V Educators of Colorado; John Echo-Hawk, Pawnee, Director of Native American Rights Fund; Debra Blacketter, Ogalala Sioux; Susan and Glenn Minor, teacher and trader, Rough Rock, Arizona; Sally Begay; Galena Dick; Lorinda Gray; Afton Sells; Rita Wagner; Gloria Sells; Linda Teller; and the teachers and many friends at Rough Rock Community School.

May you always have Beauty Ahead, Beauty Behind, Beauty Underneath, Beauty Above, and Beauty All Around you and Always Speak with Beauty.

—Mr. Alfred W. Yazzie

PREFACE

We are all children of our Mother Earth,
brothers and sisters to each other.

What should social studies teachers teach about Native Americans? Simply stated, we should teach about Native American peoples as they really were and as they really are. Social studies teachers need to be historically accurate and fair, as well as sensitive to the contemporary needs and concerns of a dominated, often displaced, and threatened people. They need to be acutely aware of the moral and ethical values inherent in the study of the historical and contemporary lives of Native Americans. Curriculum materials and instructional aids should be free of racism and ethnocentrism. Teachers must recognize the contributions of Native Americans throughout the curriculum and each and every teacher must be cognizant of the negative effects of stereotypes, and the prejudice and discrimination rampant in our treaties, policies, and government and public practices in the treatment of and interaction with Native peoples.

Another equally important role social studies teachers can logically assume is that of teaching their colleagues about the rightful place of Native American peoples in our history and contemporary society, about their significant contributions, and about their struggles to maintain their cultural ways, regain their land, and preserve and enhance their dignified presence in contemporary America. This includes portions of the curriculum that extend beyond social studies education such as ensuring that Indian authors are represented in American literature courses, analyzing current films, videos, and books for negative stereotypes, and screening school Thanksgiving celebrations for ethnocentricity.

We strongly believe that social studies teachers in elementary and secondary schools throughout the nation have the obligation to teach about Native American people with accuracy and respect and in ways that acknowledge the place that racism and ethnocentrism have played in determining our history and our understanding of ourselves and others. We also believe that the future can indeed improve for Native Americans and that there is faith that the United States of America will provide for liberty and justice for all.

This bulletin is intended to provide direct and practical support for elementary and secondary teachers who teach about Native Americans and who share our respect and concern for the indigenous people of our nation.

Not apologists for the plight of Indians past or present, [we] are committed to remembering real Indian history while working toward a proud Indian future. (Herold 1978)

Karen D. Harvey
Lisa D. Harjo
Jane K. Jackson

Come sit with me, and let us smoke the Pipe of Peace in Understanding.
Let us Touch. Let us, each to the other, be a Gift as is the Buffalo. Let us be
Meat to Nourish each other, that we all may Grow. Sit here with me each
of you as you are in your own Perceiving of yourself, as Mouse, Wolf,
Coyote, Weasel, Fox, or Prairie Bird. Let me see though your Eyes. Let us
Teach each other here in this Great Lodge of the People, this Sun Dance, of
each of the Ways on this Great Medicine Wheel, our Earth.

—Hyemeyohsts Storm, 1972

CHAPTER ONE
INTRODUCTION

As I listened to the Native American speakers share their experience as Indians, I became humbled. In a very positive sense, I became aware of my inability to understand truly what it means to be a Native American. My role as a teacher became clearer to me. Rather than looking to be the "expert" about Colorado Indians, I need to be the student of the Native Americans. Teaching knowledge and factual information is important but even more important is teaching a reverence and respect for the Indian way of life.

—Teacher, Plains Indians Institute, Denver 1989

INTRODUCTION

As this teacher so thoughtfully shared, teaching about Native Americans is not nearly as uncomplicated or straightforward as it may seem initially. It is, in fact, a truly complex challenge for many social studies teachers. Let us look briefly at some of the issues—then confront the challenge by presenting a workable, sensible model and some examples.

The first issue is to recognize the depth and breadth of the task. To learn about and teach about Native Americans is very similar to learning about and teaching about Europe—at least in the broad sweep of time as well as in its geography, cultures, governments, languages, and economics. Consider this brief list of facts:

- Native American cultures span perhaps twenty or more millennia—from before written history to today (and tomorrow).

- Most Native American history is tentative, speculative, and written by European or Anglo-American explorers or scholars. Furthermore, diseases carried to North America by European immigrants decimated many tribes, entirely destroyed others, and resulted in losing the rich oral histories of Native peoples.

- Physical environments that influenced the development of ancient and contemporary Native American cultures included Arctic tundra, woodlands, deserts, Mesoamerican jungles, prairies, plateaus, plains, swamps, and mountains.

- Linguists believe that at least 200 languages and perhaps many more were spoken in North America before European contact. These languages, often not of the same language family, were as different from each other as Mandarin Chinese is different from Greek. Scholars estimate that about 73 language families existed in North America at the time of European contact. Today, about 250 languages are spoken, some by only a few people.

- Currently, there are about 505 federally recognized tribes in the United States and 304 Federal Indian Reservations.

- There is no one federal or tribal definition that establishes a person's identity as an Indian. Government agencies use different criteria for determining who is an Indian. Similarly, tribal groups have varying requirements for determining tribal membership.

All but the most cursory study will reveal that the subject is vast, complicated, diverse, and difficult. Where do you as a teacher start? How do you focus? What is accurate? Finally, and most important, what is worthy of teaching?

The second issue concerns the desirability of a standard or uniform content or curriculum. Although it would be convenient for some teachers and would interest others, a bulletin presenting *what* to teach is not realistic or desirable for classroom teachers. Furthermore, it would be constraining and arrogantly disdainful of local issues and needs. It is inappropriate to expect teachers throughout the nation to adopt a single, national curriculum regarding Native Americans. Each geographical and political region and each classroom teacher has differing expectations, resources, and requirements. Teachers also have individual personal interests and varying levels of professional expertise. For example, teachers in the Southeast will want to teach entirely different content than teachers in the Northwest. Local history differs from place to place, local problems are unique, and resources available to particular schools vary.

Finally, availability of information and resources for curriculum development generally is not a major problem for most teachers. Abundant books and other resources are available for the teacher, at any grade level, to create meaningful units of study about Native Americans. Specifically, the difficulty lies in identifying a focus for study, and sifting through the myriad of available resources for information and activities that are accurate and genuinely useful.

The challenge then is how to select significant content with a focus that will interest students, demonstrate respect for Native Americans, is historically accurate, is congruent with local curriculum needs, and resources and, is organized into meaningful, cohesive social science learning.

The model that provides the organization and structure upon which we base this bulletin is simple, clear, and suggests a way for teachers to meet this challenge. It acknowledges the obligation of educators to select specific content for their students, it discourages the very real danger of teaching a collection of unrelated, yet interesting, facts by developing major social science concepts throughout the K-12 curriculum. It encourages teachers to select appropriate content from all major geographical-cultural regions and time periods (fig. 1.1). The concept-based model is not restricted to a particular culture area or historical period. It will be equally useful as a guide for teachers at all grade levels.

To demonstrate the flexibility and usefulness of this organizing model, we have developed sample lesson plans developed in the chapters that follow for each of the concept clusters presented in the model that should help individual teachers or curriculum developers adapt the requirements of their department, school, district, or state to a sound social studies curriculum about Native Americans. For contrast and cohesiveness, the *content* of the lesson plans has been drawn primarily from two cultural areas, the **Southwest** and the **Northeast**. The lesson plans should demonstrate the model while stimulating the interest and imagination of social studies teachers. Each plan, regardless of level and specific regional content, should contain ideas that resourceful

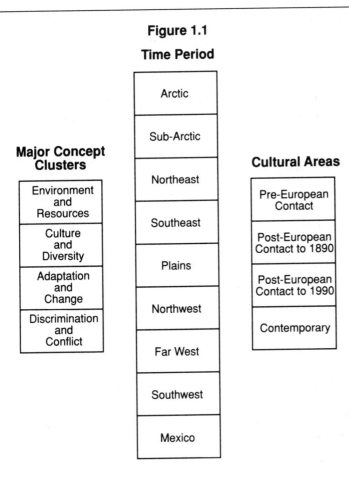

Figure 1.1

Time Period

Arctic

Sub-Arctic

Northeast

Southeast

Plains

Northwest

Far West

Southwest

Mexico

Major Concept Clusters

Environment and Resources

Culture and Diversity

Adaptation and Change

Discrimination and Conflict

Cultural Areas

Pre-European Contact

Post-European Contact to 1890

Post-European Contact to 1990

Contemporary

teachers can adapt or expand in a variety of ways. The plans should be considered as suggestions or possibilities rather than recipes.

TEACHING MAJOR CONCEPTS AND SOCIAL SCIENCE GENERALIZATIONS

CONCEPTS

"If you are committed to helping students develop their thinking skills and learn the structure of the social science disciplines, you must teach concepts" (Woolever and Scott 1988).

A concept is a word or phrase that is used to label a group of similar people, things, events, actions, or ideas. Teaching concepts helps students organize and make sense of their world and their school experiences and is basic to higher-level thinking and understanding. As mental constructs, concepts are building blocks necessary to make large and powerful generalizations about the social world.

Major social science concepts emphasized in this approach to teaching about Native Americans help to guide teachers away from transmitting snippets of interesting information about our indigenous cultures and toward a deep understanding of historical events and ways of life and of contemporary issues. Unexamined facts or superficial activities can

perpetuate myths and stereotypes; whereas facts taught to assist students in forming concepts and generalizations give them great power to understand historical events and predict and apprehend new events, issues, or facts.

Who is not familiar with the picture or cartoon of the Indian person sending smoke signals? As an example of the *concept* of stereotyping, this is a useful caricature. As an example of the following *generalization*, it is also appropriate: Technological development affects Indian cultures.

However, as a cultural *fact*, taught in isolation, it is trivial at best and probably detrimental to understanding Indian peoples.

GENERALIZATIONS

A generalization is a statement of relationship between two or more concepts. Generalizations are commonly called principles and are considered to be the major and most powerful ideas that help students to organize and make sense of the array of facts and personal experiences they encounter.

Native American culture is rich, diverse, and inherently interesting to young and old alike. In order to avoid the superficial and quaint in studying these indigenous people, we must select facts carefully so that they assist students in constructing significant knowledge—social science concepts and generalizations (fig. 1.2).

A SPIRAL CURRICULUM

Can we create an entire K-12 curriculum around the study of just four major concept clusters? The answer to this significant question is a resounding yes!

Concepts with great power and with a hierarchical nature can be developed at increasingly higher levels and in greater depth as students acquire understanding. The intent is to help students gain ever-increasing knowledge and sophistication about these identified concepts. Every concept may not be taught at each grade level, or in all units, but should recur throughout the entire K-12 social studies curriculum.

Realistically, understanding major concepts and principles of social science content is a developmental process—it does not occur after one lesson or even one year. An organized curriculum presents developmentally appropriate content that helps students to construct significant meaning from their learning experiences throughout their school years. Content about Native Americans, or any other culture that is unconnected to other learning and experiences, tends to remain merely interesting trivia.

The spiral curriculum can be visually expressed by concept strands that run throughout the curriculum and are dealt with in evolving depth and complexity (fig. 1.3).

MORAL, ETHICAL, AND VALUE ISSUES

Because factual knowledge without ethical understanding is insufficient for developing active citizens in a just and

---

Figure 1.2. Teaching About Native Americans: A Concept-Based Curriculum

Concept Clusters	Organizing Generalization
Environment and Resources	The physical environment and natural resources of a region affect how people meet their basic needs of food, clothing, and shelter. Culture is related to geographic location and to the particular time in which people live.
Culture and Diversity	Culture is comprised of a human-made system of artifacts, beliefs, and patterns of behavior that enables people to meet their needs in their physical and social environment.
	Cultures use a diversity of means to attain similar goals and to satisfy human needs.
	Individuals become human by learning the culture of their group. There are many ways of being human.
	An individual's culture strongly influences his or her behavior and values.
Adaptation and Change	Culture change takes place when diverse cultures come in contact.
	Every culture consists of a variety of borrowed cultural elements.
	Culture is an integrated whole. Changes in one part are reflected in all its components.
	Conflict sometimes leads to social change.
Conflict and Discrimination	Conflict usually results when people from different cultures and subcultures interact.
	Groups are often the victims of discrimination and prejudice because of age, gender, sexual orientation, racial, religious, or cultural differences.

---

democratic society, the content we present and learning activities we pursue should emphasize decision making, critical thinking, and valuing. We would hope for an enlightened and bold citizenship that willingly confronts such issues as preserving Indian land, restoring fishing and hunting rights, protecting archaeological sites, displaying Indian religious items in our museums, and granting Indian self-determination.

Another useful way of looking at the moral, ethical, and value issues in curriculum is to distinguish between the mastery curriculum and the organic curriculum (Glatthorn 1987). The basic mastery curriculum meets two criteria: It is essential for all students, and it requires careful structuring. In the basic mastery curriculum, the objectives are easily quantified and measured. In this bulletin, we would consider the basic mastery goals to be the social science generalizations with the instructional objectives designed by individual teachers or districts.

In the organic curriculum, however, the objectives do not lend themselves to focused teaching and careful measuring. These objectives have to do with attitudes, values, and appreciations and are primarily taught by the attitudes and behaviors modeled by teachers, the climate of the school, continuing instructional reinforcement, and the everyday interactions of the people within the school. Examples of the organic curriculum would include the development of a positive self-image for all students, respect for Native American beliefs and values, and appreciation of Native American

contributions (see Lesson Plan). These value objectives are part of the organic curriculum and are reinforced *throughout* the K-12 curriculum.

Another example of both mastery and organic goals is presented in the quotation at the beginning of this chapter. "Teaching knowledge and factual information about the Indian ways of life are important [mastery] but even more important is teaching a reverence and respect for the Indian way of life [organic]."

THE CONCEPT-BASED MODEL

In using the model for guidance in planning curriculum, teachers at all levels will select one or more components from each of the three columns in the model: (1) major concepts, (2) geographic and cultural areas, and (3) historical time period. Curriculum development begins by selecting from any one column in the model. For example, a middle school teacher might elect or be required to teach a particular historical topic such as Westward Expansion. This designated time or historical period would serve as the initial step in planning; the next step would then be to identify one or more of the major concept clusters to guide the unit of study as it relates to Native Americans, such as environment and resources and change and adaptation. In this case, it is likely that the content area would focus on one or more of the nine geographic and culture areas such as the Plains and the Northeast.

Figure 1.3

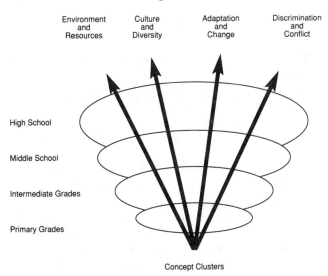

Concept Clusters

Topic: Westward Expansion

Major Concepts: environment and resources, change and adaptation

Cultural Area: Plains

Time Period: Post-European Contact to 1890

At this point, the teacher should identify knowledge (mastery), skills (including social skills and thinking skills) and value (organic) objectives. Then comes the creative part—creating, adapting, or selecting teaching and learning activities that meet the learning needs of your students and help them achieve the identified objectives.

INTEGRATING CONTENT INTO REQUIRED CURRICULA

Very few teachers plan specific units or courses about Native Americans. The exception undoubtedly would be in states or areas that are on or adjacent to large federal reservations, many 3d or 4th grade classrooms when studying geographic regions, and perhaps high schools that emphasize ethnic studies. Another exception might include materials developed for such special events as part of state or city historical celebrations. Throughout the country, most teaching about Native Americans is integrated into other units or courses of study—sometimes with a significant focus and, at other times, with merely a casual mention. Although you may not teach a specific unit or course about Native Americans, we certainly believe that the use of the model will enable teachers to move beyond tipis, Pocahontas, and pow-wows to the integration of significant content in such courses or parts of courses as:

- Holidays (specifically Thanksgiving Day, Columbus Day, and Native American Day)
- Regions of the world
- State history

- American History
- United States Government
- Contemporary issues

This is perhaps the time to acknowledge that although we have written this bulletin to assist teachers of social studies, we would encourage teachers in other parts of the curriculum to teach about Native Americans. Many elementary, middle school, and high school teachers work in teaching teams and are jointly responsible for the entire curriculum for a particular group of students. Native American art and literature have unique contributions for studying not only Native American people and cultures but also for studying American art and literature.

Literature and art provide profound opportunities to walk in another's shoes—or moccasins—and understand the heart and soul of a people and thus contribute significantly to social science education. However, they are worth studying simply as great American art and literature. It would be remiss for those who teach English, language arts, art appreciation, or humanities courses not to include the contributions of Native Americans. These aspects of Native American culture should be taught in classes other than social studies. As aesthetic products of indigenous cultures, our lives are enriched by their special beauty.

USING LANGUAGE OF RESPECT

Language has power—power to teach by inference, insinuation, and modeling; power to lead; power to confer or destroy respect and dignity. Certain terms are known to be derogatory and destructive, whereas others, with an equally negative connotation, are less well-known or so widely accepted that their usage is considered somehow benign or acceptable. Although Native people often differ in their understanding and acceptance of some terms, it seems important to teach with language of respect. In this bulletin, we have chosen the term *Native Americans*. It is a commonly used term, easily understood, reasonably accurate, and usually accepted by most North American indigenous peoples.

The only acceptable terms for referring to Native Americans are the following:

Indians: A common term, acceptable to most, but not all native people. Can be confused with people native to India.

Native Americans: Acceptable to most, but not all native people. Implies that they are not immigrants but have *always* been here.

American Indians: Reasonably acceptable, but confusing as to heritage. Are they citizens of India, living in America?

Indigenous Peoples: An academic term which is perhaps the most accurate reference to Indian peoples. Can sound awkward at times. Not often used by Indian people.

All others such as the following, regardless of their common usage, should be avoided:

Injuns: A relic of old movies and an unacceptable term;

Skins: A frequently used, slang term used among young, contemporary Native Americans; Red Man: There are better descriptions of all human beings than those of supposed skin color; Chief: Often used to denote older Native American males—usually used as a stereotype. Most tribes have tribal chairmen or chairwomen; Squaw: Derogatory term that should not be used; Papoose: A general term that has racist or stereotypical inference. Baby is acceptable; Brave: Often used to apply to all Native American young men of courage and valor. No longer very useful as a contemporary term; Warrior: Usually used as a general term for Native American men. If used to describe a man of courage and leadership in conflict or battle, it is acceptable; Redskins: Commonly used as a school or team symbol, it is a very stereotypical term and suggests that a group of people can be used as mascots or that certain cultural characteristics can be parodied.

STRIVING FOR ACCURACY AND AUTHENTICITY

Previously, we mentioned that much of the oral tradition of Native Americans was lost when disease destroyed so many indigenous people. European explorers, traders, artists, and scholars recorded early accounts of native cultures with their own cultural and historical perspectives. These circumstances are complicated by an incomplete archaeological story. Consequently, it is difficult to achieve accuracy and authenticity. Recognizing that educators have limited time available for adding materials to the curriculum, we offer the following suggestions:

* Study—develop authoritative information by taking classes offered by colleges, universities, and museums.
* Read—obtain a variety of perspectives on any given tribe, incident, or period of time.
* Consult—seek the views of Native American authors, historians, artists, and tribal members.
* Teach—emphasize the effects of historical bias, and the existence of varying perspectives.

SELECTING LEARNING ACTIVITIES

Gone are the days when teaching was synonymous with lecturing. Learning activities today must reflect what we know about human development and human learning. In other words, what can teachers do to bring what is *taught* and what is *learned* together to achieve the desired results? We offer the following checklist as a practical reminder of the qualities of effective learning activities:

* Require active rather than passive student involvement.
* Present significant content relevant to students' needs and interests.
* Engage students in independent, small, and large group work.
* Use a variety of instructional materials.
* Use a variety of teaching and learning strategies.

* Provide opportunities for the functional use of basic skills including thinking skills, social skills, and valuing skills.
* Create opportunities for communication and aesthetic expression.
* Provide opportunities for exploring fundamental democratic principles.
* Provide opportunities to explore and develop personal, social, moral, and ethical values.
* Invite students to engage in meaningful social inquiry and action.

Finally, we offer another checklist that stipulates what we think should not be taught about Native Americans. As redundant as it may seem, it is necessary to remind ourselves of the importance of examining traditional and comfortable ways of teaching, of being alert to the effect of our own experiences and personal perspective on the professional decisions we make, and translating our professed interests and concerns into strong, positive teaching and learning strategies in our classrooms.

NATIVE AMERICANS: WHAT NOT TO TEACH

by June Sark Heinrich
(source unknown)

* Do not use alphabet cards that say A is for apple, B is for ball, and I is for Indian.
* Do not talk about Indians as though they belong to the past.
* Do not talk about "them" and "us."
* Do not lump all Native Americans together.
* Do not expect Native Americans to look like Hollywood movie Indians.
* Do not let TV stereotypes go unchallenged.
* Do not let students get the impression that a few "brave" Europeans defeated millions of "Indian savages" in battle.
* Do not teach that Native Americans are just like other racial and ethnic minorities.
* Do not assume that Native American children are well acquainted with their heritage.
* Do not let students think that native ways of life have no meaning today.

References

Glatthorn, A. A. *Curriculum Renewal.* Alexandria, Va.: Association for Supervision and Curriculum Development, 1987.

Miles, M. *Annie and the Old One.* Boston, Mass.: Little, Brown and Company, 1971.

Woolever, R., and K. P. Scott. *Active Learning in Social Studies: Promoting Cognitive and Social Growth.* Glenview, Ill.: Scott Foresman, 1988.

Lesson Plan

TEACHING ABOUT NATIVE AMERICANS: A SAMPLE LESSON

Grade Level: Primary to Intermediate (Grades 3 and 4)

Basic Concepts: Culture and diversity

Organizing Generalization: An individual's culture strongly influences his or her behavior and values.

Culture Area: Southwest Region

Time Period: Post-European Contact to 1990.

Background:

In the study of the Navajo, students have learned about such things as traditional hogans, sheep herding, and artwork, including weaving. They have also studied the physical environment of the reservation and some of the spiritual beliefs of the Navajo. The wonderful story of *Annie and the Old One* (Miles 1971) will help link these cultural elements to the real world of Navajo children and Navajo values, behavior, and way of life.

Objectives:

Knowledge (Content): Students will

1. state in their own words why they believe Annie acted as she did. Their discussion should reflect an awareness of her love for her grandmother, her reluctance to face her grandmother's impending death, her developing understanding of the Navajo belief in the circle of life, and her subsequent change in behavior;

2. relate Annie's family and feelings for them to their own families and experiences; and

3. discuss the relationship between values and behavior, and give some examples from their own lives.

Skills: Students will

1. practice making inferences—"Why was the weaving stick important to Annie and her grandmother?"

Values: (Organic) Students will

1. gain understanding and appreciation of another culture's beliefs regarding death; and

2. begin to understand that behavior, including their own, is related to values and that their way of life (culture) helps to determine their values and their behavior.

Activities:

1. Read aloud *Annie and the Old One* (Miles 1971).

2. Class discussion:

   a. "Annie's Navajo world was good" (3). What do we already know about Annie's Navajo world? Answers are likely to be related to environment, family, and ways of life. Illustrations in the book are excellent and will help students understand the relationship between the environment and way of life. Solicit ideas about what Navajo people believe is important. The story gives examples of the importance of some items (weaving stick, sheep, etc.), people, and basic belief systems.

   b. Give some examples of how Annie was trying to keep her mother from finishing the rug.

   c. Why was Annie trying to keep her mother from finishing the rug? Discuss the following statements:

      • "My children, when the new rug is taken from the loom, I will go to Mother Earth."

      • "Your grandmother is one of those who lives in harmony with all nature—with earth, coyote, birds in the sky. They know more than many will ever learn. Those Old Ones know."

   d. Navajo people believe in the circle of life. Discuss the following statements:

      • "The sun comes up from the edge of earth in the morning. It returns to the edge of earth in the evening. Earth, from which good things come for the living creatures on it. Earth, to which all creatures finally go."

      • "The sun rose but it also set." "The cactus did not bloom forever." "She would always be a part of the earth, just as her grandmother had always been, just as her grandmother would always be, always and forever."

   e. What does this mean, "…Annie was breathless with the wonder of it"?

   f. How did Annie's behavior change? Why?

   g. Can you think of any beliefs that you and your family have that help you decide how to act? The teacher should record these ideas on a chart or chalkboard.

   h. Encourage students to summarize, in their own words, the relationship between culture, values, and behavior.

EXTENSION

Depending on the focus and length of the unit of study, the teacher might want to extend this lesson to helping students understand the behavior of Native American people in other historical periods.

Evaluation:

Students will be able to state the generalization in their own words.

Materials and Resources:

Miles, M. *Annie and the Old One*. Boston, Mass.: Little, Brown and Company, 1971.

Navajo rug, model of a Navajo loom, and weaving stick, if possible.

CHAPTER TWO
ENVIRONMENT AND RESOURCES

God created the Indian Country and it was like he spread out a big blanket. He put the Indians on it. They were created here in this Country, truly honest, and that was the time this river started to run. Then God created fish in this river and put deer in the mountains and made laws through which has come the increase of fish and game. Then the Creator gave us Indians Life; we walked, and as soon as we saw the game and fish we knew they were made for us. For the women, God made roots and berries to gather, and the Indians grew and multiplied as a people...

—Chief Weninock of the Yakimas (McLuhan 1971)

ENVIRONMENT AND RESOURCES

Physical Environment: The natural physical surroundings including land forms, water bodies, climate, soils, native plants, and animals.

Natural Resources: The animals, plants, soils, and minerals in their physical environment that people have learned to use.

Habitats: Environments in which people and other living things live.

In the latter part of the 20th century, the dominant culture in the United States has become increasingly aware of the environmental problems created by a particular system of values. Ways of reversing these effects can be devised only when these attitudes, values, and behaviors begin to change.

Native Americans lived for thousands of years in harmony and balance with their natural surroundings and maintained the health of the provider elements of the Earth. Perhaps the wisdom and values that allowed them to maintain that balance and live fully and healthfully will be useful for us now as we explore viable ways to recover the health of the planet.

By the early 20th century, the use and abuse of the natural resources of the land had changed the balance and the way Native peoples had lived for 10,000 to 12,000 years. In this chapter, we will examine how, until the 1900s, Native Americans adapted to and made use of what they found in their natural environment. The environmental realities that surround a group affect not only the physical existence of the people, but also shape their culture, including their values and attitudes and their concept of their place in the world.

We will examine how Native Americans have traditionally used naturally occurring materials in their habitats as primary resources and how the physical environment helped to create world views and value systems that have sustained cultures for thousands of years in North America. In preparing to study these sections, teachers and students should consult and have handy a good atlas and the teacher should mount a large physical map of North America in the classroom. In the atlas examine maps of North America that show landforms, climate, natural vegetation, and water resources. Compare these maps with each other to see how they coincide generally with the regions that follow.

GENERALIZATIONS

Native Americans used naturally occurring materials as resources to meet their basic needs for food, clothing, and shelter.

The natural environment provided general guidelines for the development of North American native cultures. Some research workers have identified approximately nine geographic regions in which unique patterns of culture have developed. [The number of identifiable regions may differ from source to source depending upon the criteria used for defining them. Some research workers use sub-regions as separate regions such as California, Great Basin, and Plateau (Columbia and Fraser) whereas others group them together as one region—the Far West.]

North America might be divided into nine geographical regions whose unique location, landforms, climate, and natural resources have influenced the particular cultures and traditional ways of Native American life (Kopper 1986). We will use these nine regions consistently throughout this bulletin to maintain clarity and focus for the reader (figs. 2.1, 2.2). Beginning with the Arctic Region and continuing south to the Mexican Region, we will highlight the major geographic and cultural differences and similarities between and among these regions.

ARCTIC REGION

LOCATION AND CLIMATE

The Arctic region extends from the Aleutian Islands, along the western coast of Alaska, to the southern coast of the Arctic Ocean, and eastward to the Atlantic Ocean (figs. 2.1, 2.2). The most outstanding characteristic of the region is its harsh climate. Ice covers most of the region in the form of ice floes and ice packs on the water and glaciers on the higher elevations. Permafrost prevents the development of deep roots for any food plants that might help animals or humans survive.

RESOURCES

Arctic inhabitants have depended on the available animals for survival. A variety of birds, sea mammals, fresh water fish, bears, and some salt water fish, had been plentiful until Europeans arrived. Natural vegetation was limited by the harsh climate.

WAYS OF LIFE

The balance between prey and predators is delicate and the human population is required to adjust to that balance. All articles of clothing, household tools, and all the tools and weapons that the inhabitants required for hunting and transporting could be found in the bone, sinew, and hides of Arctic animals. Since animals do not always hunt in a predictable pattern, the people who depended on them to survive, had to travel after them. Consequently, the people of this region became some of the greatest travelers of North America, traversing the continent's 6,000 miles (9,600 km) from west to east in their migratory search for the necessities of life.

Because of their complete dependence upon the animals that sustained them, the people revered them as sacred for

Figure 2.1

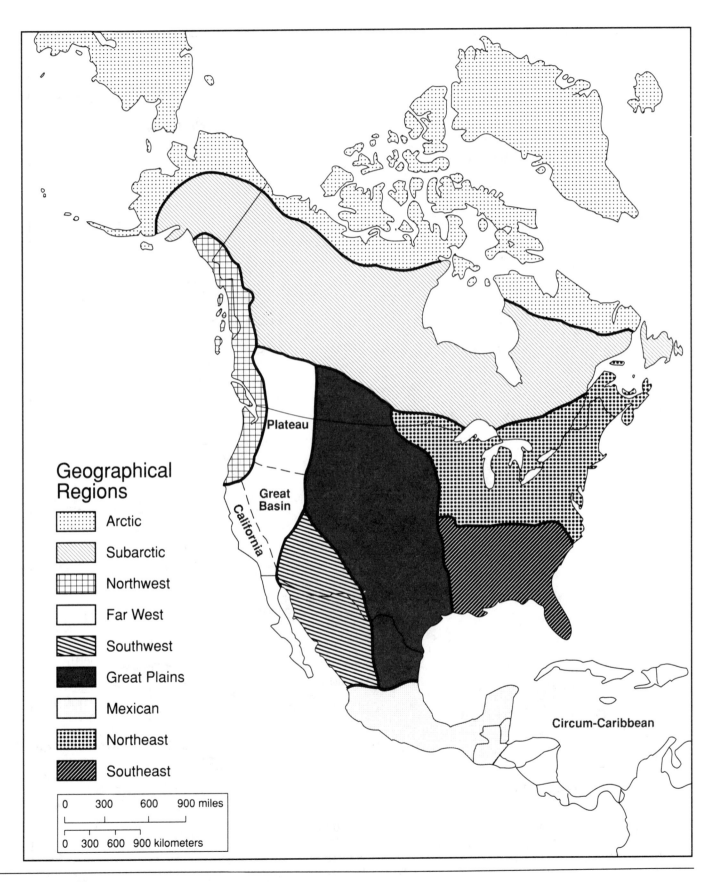

Geographical Regions

- Arctic
- Subarctic
- Northwest
- Far West
- Southwest
- Great Plains
- Mexican
- Northeast
- Southeast

Plateau

Great Basin

California

Circum-Caribbean

0   300   600   900 miles

0   300 600 900 kilometers

Figure 2.2

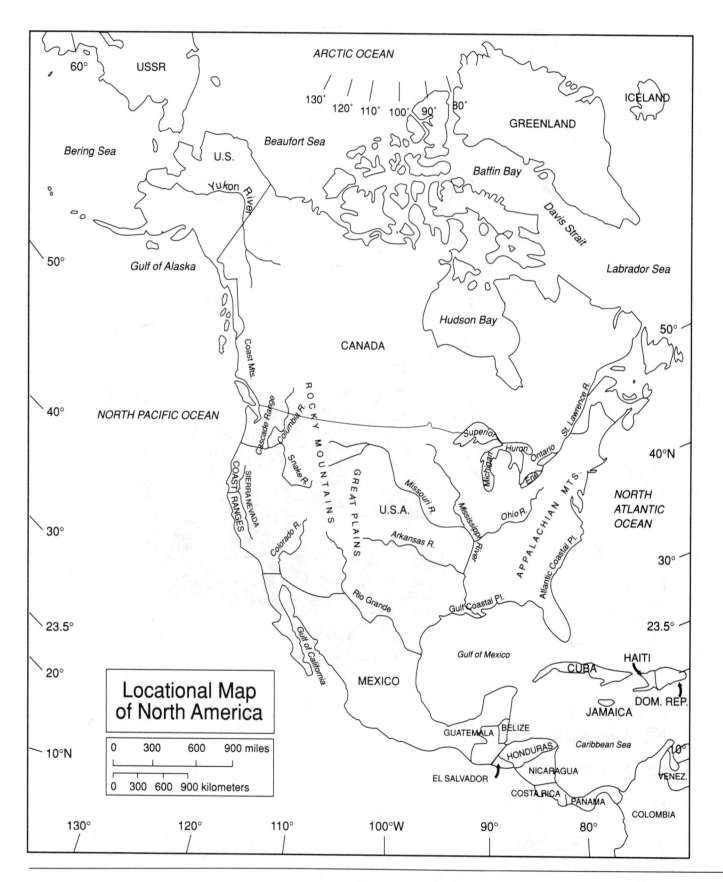

Locational Map of North America

their existence. Ceremony and respect for life was part of the everyday life rituals of Arctic people. The spaciousness of the land and the freedom to travel was fundamental in their view of life and reality. These patterns endured from time immemorial because their ways of life had worked and they trusted these patterns as ways to live.

Over the millennia, Arctic inhabitants have maintained consistent ways of life and have endeavored to balance available resources and population to conserve the life-giving elements of nature. Nevertheless, the harsh environment exacted a stern toll and served as a constant reminder of its limitations to the inhabitants. The balance, however, has been disturbed by several factors. The arrival of outsiders who came to hunt for sport or for commercial profit depleted the supply of animals faster than they could reproduce. The introduction of modern technology, particularly the gun and the motor, has made hunting easier than in the past, but it has also changed the way things have been done traditionally. Recent generations have lost the old skills and now must depend on the outside world for modern hunting equipment.

SUBARCTIC REGION

LOCATION AND CLIMATE

The Subarctic Region is the largest region of the continent. It extends for 2 million square miles (3.218 million square km) from Alaska and eastward across Canada to the Maritime Provinces on the Atlantic Coast (figs. 2.1, 2.2). Its climatic characteristics are less severe than the Arctic Region, but at its northern reaches, it is still extremely harsh. Most of the region is underlain by permafrost that can support only stunted vegetation, mostly mosses, lichens, and stunted conifers and hardwoods. It also prohibits agriculture. Areas free of permafrost have such a short growing season that very few plants can be cultivated. The southern sections support a boreal forest or taiga of largely coniferous and some broadleaf deciduous trees that grow slowly because of the poor soils and the brief frost-free season.

RESOURCES

The greatest assets of the region are the caribou, moose, bear, beaver, small rodents, and fresh water fish in the rivers and the inland glacial lakes. The bone, sinew, and hides of the large animals provide the major portion of diet, as well as the materials for sleds, runners, snowshoes, and leather for clothing. The forests provide the habitat for the wildlife as well as the birch bark for canoes. Because of the nomadic way of life in early days, little lumber was used for permanent dwellings. The lakes and rivers provided the avenues for travel in the warm seasons as well as in the winter.

WAYS OF LIFE

Because the region is so vast, and survival so difficult, the inhabitants lived in small bands and traveled in search of game. As a result, no complex systems of economic or political life developed. It was not a matter of the inhabitants of this region being incapable of complexity, as some would like to assume. It was simply a matter of having no need for a complex social organization. Consequently, the people of the Subarctic retained the old patterns of survival that worked for them for so many thousands of years. When a way of life makes sense and it works, there is little incentive to alter it. When the sacred becomes a part of that life pattern, it cannot be changed or the entire world view is shattered. In the past century, however, some changes have occurred as technologies intruded and supplanted the old ways. The loss of stability has been disastrous to the traditional way of life, much as it has in the Arctic Region.

NORTHEAST REGION

LOCATION AND CLIMATE

The Northeast is a region with more diversity of climate and topography than the Arctic and the Subarctic Regions. It extends, in the eastern part of the continent, from the southern boundary of the Subarctic to the Ohio Valley and from the Atlantic coast to the Missouri River (figs. 2.1, 2.2). It has been inhabited for at least 12,000 years. The area possesses climatic variety ranging from harsh winters and cool summers in the north to the mild winters and hot, humid, summers of the south.

RESOURCES

Because of these diverse climatic conditions, the frost-free seasons permit the growth of trees for a variety of timber as well as for many species of food plants. Before the arrival of the Europeans, the area was heavily forested and where farming was done, only small plots were cleared as they were needed. Good soil exists consistently throughout the area and rainfall is usually plentiful to allow cultivation of edible plants for human consumption as well as natural pasture for wildlife. Prior to the domestication of seeds for farming, a hunter/gatherer economy prevailed. The first plants that were domesticated were the sunflower and the squash. Eventually the people domesticated other seed-bearing plants and devised methods of preserving them. Along the coast, people learned to fish and fish became a staple in their diet.

In the Lake Superior area, ample supplies of copper ore were used to produce tools. There is evidence that the tribes traded with other tribes as far away as the Rocky Mountains especially in a volcanic rock, obsidian, found in the northeastern part of the region. Obsidian was used to make cutting tools. Shells from the coast are found inland, indicating trade up and down the rivers east of the Appalachian Mountains. Birch bark was plentiful for use in building canoes in the north and dugout canoes were common in the southern region. The technology for building canoes to ply the rivers made trade possible. Trading permitted more goods and a greater variety in daily life for the people in each part of the region than would have been possible had they relied solely on their own resources.

WAYS OF LIFE

Trees in the abundant forests produced timber to build permanent homes. The community of the Longhouse became common in parts of the region. Obviously, people living in common quarters need to work out ways to deal with each other in more complex ways than nomadic people living in small groups. The Iroquois Confederacy developed one of the most complex systems of government that became the prototype of democracy. Many of the concepts embodied in the Constitution of the United States originated in this confederacy. For example, the Iroquois Confederacy provided for the equality of women, and a way for nations to come together in peace and to settle differences and difficulties. The Great Law of Peace of the Iroquois has been a major contributor to our democratic form of government and will be a topic for later discussion.

SOUTHEAST REGION

LOCATION AND CLIMATE

The Southeast Region extends from the Atlantic coast west to the Mississippi River and from the Ohio River south to the Gulf of Mexico (figs. 2.1, 2.2). It is a region that also has been inhabited for 12,000 years. At one time it had the most complex society in North America. The region's climates range from humid, continental interiors to the humid, subtropical of the coastal areas. As a result, conditions were favorable for producing a variety and abundance of vegetation for human and animal consumption. Early people were hunters and gatherers and they depended on a variety of nuts, seeds, and berries as well as game, which included deer, fish, rodents, raccoons, and birds. The earliest domesticated plants were corn and beans. When the farmers exhausted an agricultural site, people of the region simply moved on. The natural vegetation grew back and helped the soil to replenish itself.

RESOURCES

Extensive forests provided the materials for building permanent settlements. The people of this region developed complex social and political organizations as their ability to grow and store more food improved. They used stone tools, and they also produced pottery. They traveled in dugout canoes on rivers and they traded with others nearly 1,000 miles (1,609 km) away for needed goods.

WAYS OF LIFE

Archaeologists discovered huge mounds of earth in many locations in the Southeast Region. These mounds seem to have been elaborate burial sites for the members of the higher class and indicate the presence of socially stratified societies. Extravagant use of jewelry and other artifacts accompanying the bodies suggest widespread affluence in the region. As people became materially secure and sophisticated, they traded with people who possessed things they wanted in order to maintain the standard of living they enjoyed.

The climatic and landform differences from the Arctic to the Southeast, dramatically demonstrate the influence of physical geography on culture. Because the early people of the Southeast Region had so many advantages in providing for their survival and an abundance of materials for doing so, they also had the time and ease to develop a highly complex and affluent way of life. Yet, these mound builders disappeared and were succeeded by what non-Indians refer to as the Five Civilized Tribes (Cherokee, Creek, Seminole, Choctaw, and Chickasaw).

We can find some legacies from the "Ancient Ones" to the Five Tribes who succeeded them. Both practiced the same hierarchical pattern of government and similar agriculture and technology. These Five Civilized Tribes, however, were the victims of a massive governmental removal to Oklahoma in the early 1830s. All the familiar natural resources, including abundant rainfall, fertile soil, and the presence of vast forests were taken from them during a span of a few years and they were expected to carry on life as they knew it in completely alien surroundings. Without time to adapt to the loss of those familiar things that they had taken for granted, the government expected the tribes to take on new ways of life, new values, and accept many restrictions to their freedom. All five tribes had to develop new ways to survive amidst these changes. The Cherokee of Georgia adopted very different ways of living in Oklahoma from that which they knew in Georgia.

PLAINS REGION

LOCATION AND CLIMATE

The region is the most easily defined from a topographical perspective coinciding with the Great Plains physiographic region. It extends from the Missouri and Mississippi River system on the east to the Rocky Mountains on the west, and from the Gulf of Mexico northward to southern Canada (figs. 2.1, 2.2). It is an area dominated by grasslands. Because of the vastness of the area, the concept of space for the inhabitants is different from that of those in the forested regions of the East. The tributaries of the Mississippi flow eastward from the Rockies and enter the main system at intervals from north to south. Although they were navigable, there is little evidence that the Plains people used the rivers for transportation. It seems that they functioned mainly as boundaries to separate the territorial hunting grounds of different tribes.

RESOURCES

The Rocky Mountains capture precipitation from eastward moving Pacific storm systems and produce a rain-shadow for the western plains that results in a semi-arid climate west of the 100th meridian of longitude. Grasses that have adapted to the lack of rainfall, supported vast herds of buffalo, elk, goats, sheep, wolves, bear, and varieties of birds. Because of the aridity, agriculture did not became viable in the early days, except in the eastern area where higher annual rainfall from storms originating in the Gulf of Mexico permitted a combination of farming, gathering, and hunting. Permanent dwellings made of sod fringed the eastern edges of the Plains where this mixed economy existed, and these particular people followed a semi-nomadic way of life.

This climate, as well as the vastness of the region, provided the inhabitants with a way of life unique in North America. In fact, it is the Plains Indian tribes that now serve as the stereotypical "Indian." As the seasons changed, the Plains Indians pursued from north to south the buffalo and other game so vital to their survival. Each tribe developed its particular migration patterns in pursuing the game.

Climatic patterns changed too. From about 5000-2500 B.C., a dry period evaporated the lakes, reduced water table levels, and bison almost disappeared. However, the Plains were not deserted. Other animals adapted to the dry conditions and the inhabitants depended on them for survival. Sometime after 2500 B.C. enough rain fell for the grasses needed for the buffalo's survival. The herds grew into vast numbers and there seems to have been no serious disruption of wildlife habitat since then—at least until the Europeans and the railroad arrived.

WAYS OF LIFE

Before the arrival of the Europeans, it is estimated that as many as 60 million buffalo lived on the Plains. Since the buffalo were the prime resource of the inhabitants, the nomadic patterns of the people varied with the movements of the buffalo. Not only were the buffalo the primary source of food, but the Plains people used their hides, bones, and other body parts for shelter, clothing, tools, weapons, and ornamentation. Because of this dependence, the buffalo became the focus of sacred ceremonials and proper rituals surrounded the hunt to ensure success and to provide for the regeneration of this vital animal for the following year.

Although buffalo were plentiful, they were not easy to hunt until the Spanish brought the horse to the Plains in the 16th century. The horse revolutionized life on the Plains. Now tribes could cover greater distances than ever, hunting success improved, and contact increased among the tribes. Once the Plains people had mastered the use of the horse, it became essential to their survival and altered forever their ways of life. It revolutionized their methods of warfare, and when non-Indians appeared on the Plains, they met a formidable cavalry ready to defend the space the Indians called home and believed sacred.

FAR WEST REGION

LOCATION AND CLIMATE

The Far West Region consists of the Great Basin, California, and the Columbia-Fraser Plateau (figs. 2.1, 2.2). These sub-regions are characterized by extremes of climate, making some parts of this vast area extremely difficult for human habitation. Although the Cascade-Sierra ranges display quite different environmental characteristics, they have enough in common to be included with this region.

The mountain ranges create both desert-like areas and some of the most fertile areas in North America. The California coast has the most favorable climate of these three sub-regions. The Pacific Ocean provides access to fishing, and inland, fertile soils provide lush vegetation.

RESOURCES

This region has a variety of resources. The mountains separate the Great Basin from the California coast and more resources and easier ways of life are found west of the mountains. The eastern side of the mountains is an area of sparse resources. As the huge inland lakes dried up between 5000 and 2500 B.C., they left deserts of salt flats in what is now the Great Basin. Even so, varieties of plants and small animals survived. Archaeologists found ancient grinding stones indicating that the people collected grains and seeds and ground them into flour. In addition, duck decoys found from this period infer the hunting of water birds in the lakes that remained. The people used the reeds from those lakes for making intricately-woven baskets.

On the western, or California, side of the Sierra Nevada, food was more plentiful and there was greater variety than in the Great Basin. There were nuts and berries to gather as well as deer in the forests, shellfish and seals in the sea, and fertile soil for the development of agriculture. The people also used reeds and other plants for basketry. Because the rivers all flow to the Pacific Ocean, there was easy access to the sea as well as a plentiful supply of salmon that swam upstream in the rivers each year to spawn.

WAYS OF LIFE

What binds the people of this vast region together and makes them a cultural group? They relied more on gathering than on hunting to survive and they developed hunter-gatherer ways of living. The people of the Great Basin had to travel in small bands and with as little baggage as possible to make the few resources available. Besides the seeds, grains, and birds, their diet consisted of pinon nuts, small game, and rodents. These people had two climatic patterns to follow; not only did they travel north and south, but following the frost-free season they traveled into the mountains as the snow melted in the spring and where food was available into the autumn. Then they returned to the lowlands and the south for the winter.

Because of the ease in surviving on the western side of the Cascade-Sierra ranges, the people had the leisure to develop the art of fashioning iron, shells, and soapstone into tools, weapons and ornaments.

The harshness of the desert had the same effect on the people of the eastern part of the Far West Region as the cold had on those of the Subarctic Region. The nomadic requirements prevented accumulating goods and developing complex living systems. For example, the Paiutes of the 18th and

19th century were a peaceful and nomadic people who concentrated on survival and did not compete with other people for resources until the arrival of the non-Indians in the latter half of the 19th century.

NORTHWEST REGION

LOCATION AND CLIMATE

The Northwest region is a long narrow corridor about 200 miles (320 km) wide east of the Pacific coast that extends 1,500 miles (2,414 km) from northern California northward to the Subarctic (figs. 2.1, 2.2). The ocean currents traveling north from the central California coast bring warm, moist air from the Pacific to provide a maritime climate for the region. In places, along the coasts of Oregon, Washington, British Columbia, and Alaska, 200 inch (5,080 mm) annual rainfalls produce the most northerly rainforest on earth.

RESOURCES

Because of the relative warmth and moisture, the area is heavily forested and timber is used for many items necessary for survival. Plank houses were common as permanent dwellings for the community; tools, weapons, and even fibers for clothing were derived from the various species of trees. The inhabitants built boats that could carry the materials long distances for trade along the coast.

WAYS OF LIFE

As in the Southeast Region, where necessities were easy to come by, the people of the Northwest Region had the leisure to pursue trade among the different tribes. They used shells as money. There was strict accounting of the type of shell used for exchange to prevent inflation. Because of their trade, these tribes developed similar daily patterns of living although the ways in which they developed their cultures differed. Proximity to the sea provided a wealth of dietary variety. Halibut, cod, sturgeon, oysters, and, of course, the spawning salmon were staples in the diet of the Northwest Region. Seals, whales, and otters provided skins and fat as well as meat. Consequently, the people of this region had a life of abundance and their rather easy-going attitudes about material things reflect this lack of scarcity.

For example, the potlatch became a ceremony to celebrate that very abundance. It is a feast given by a family where extravagant gifts are given to the guests and the feasting goes on for days. The wealth of the family is reflected in the way they carry this out, and the satisfaction of their guests determined status in the community.

Fishing is highly valued in Northwest Indian tribes. In the past decade, the fishing rights of the river tribes of the Northwest have been disputed in the courts. Far more significance is attached to the outcome of that struggle than whether or not someone can fish. A way of life, a value system, a thousand-year-old heritage of a people is at stake. When resources provide generously, they become sacred and part of the fabric of life.

SOUTHWEST REGION

LOCATION AND CLIMATE

As long as 10,000 years ago, people migrated to the Southwest Region. This region, located in what is now New Mexico, Arizona, and northern Mexico, is characterized by a hot, dry summer and by temperate winters (figs. 2.1, 2.2). The landscape is one of the most unusual of the continent. Rivers carve deep canyons through the deserts, mountains rise abruptly from the desert basin floors, and the vegetation is different from all the other regions. The spaciousness of the desert, like that of the Plains Region, affects the way people perceive their surroundings. The lack of water and prevalence of sunshine would quite naturally stimulate a different outlook on life than that of the Indians of the Northwest Region.

RESOURCES

Because water is so precious, it became necessary for desert people to learn to control the snowmelt and save it for crops if they wanted to live in settled communities. By 1500 B.C., they had domesticated corn, beans, squash, and cotton. Corn became the staple and, like the buffalo on the Plains, it became sacred and ceremonies developed to ensure its fertility. It is relatively easy to store things in dry climates, and so the ability to dry and store corn allowed for surpluses to accumulate.

WAYS OF LIFE

The early arrivals, the Mogollon and the Hohokam, devised ways to grow and store corn and developed very sophisticated cultures as a result. Much study has gone into the reason or reasons for their eventual disappearance from the area. Many scholars believe that the technology they developed and the population growth overburdened the environment. Perhaps a drought devastated the food supply and they had become too specialized in their patterns of living to adapt to the change.

The Anasazi, or the "Old Ones," also left a rich culture. They, too, had domesticated beans, corn, squash, turkeys, and cotton. They had developed basket-making to an art. The ruins of their communities indicate sophisticated methods of surviving and complex living arrangements, that would indicate highly developed systems of economic and political structures. They are thought to be the ancestors of the present day Hopi and Zuni people.

The Apache and Navajo did not move from the north into this region until approximately 1400 A.D. We do not know what brought them here, but they arrived after a severe drought had ended and they lived in the region deserted by the people before them. They were nomadic people and traveled in the region that they themselves created. As long as there was not a great strain on the resources, and the population remained relatively stable, little trouble developed between people in the region.

Along the Rio Grande, the Pueblo communities developed. When the Spanish arrived in the 16th century, they tried to destroy the basic elements of independence and democracy of the Pueblos in their attempt to dominate them. However, they did not succeed and these Pueblo people have remained in the same places and live much as they did when the Spanish arrived. Their life has certainly been affected by the technology and culture of the non-Indian, but they have retained much of their worldview and their values from ancient times. Because their culture has been so strongly influenced by their physical environment, the people who have remained on their ancestral lands, have kept most of their traditional ways of life and value systems. Those who were moved from their land, resources, and their way of doing things have had a difficult time maintaining their culture.

MEXICAN REGION

LOCATION AND CLIMATE

The Mexican Region is characterized by semi-tropical to tropical climates and by a varied topography that includes mountains, lowlands, and desert on the northern border that extends into what is now the United States (figs. 2.1, 2.2). It is a region of lush vegetation in the lowlands, and even the mountains are productive because of their low latitudes.

RESOURCES

Some of the earliest domestication of corn developed here as early as 8750 B.C. Also domesticated were the avocado and the chili pepper which became some of the most widely used vegetables around the world (Weatherford 1988). The seasonal rains regulate the ways of life and formed the patterns for the cultures that grew up in Mexico.

WAYS OF LIFE

The heavy seasonal and predictable rainfall created the need for drainage systems to sustain the agriculture that allowed for the people to accumulate surpluses. Building and maintaining these drainage systems required cooperative efforts. Further, as the diet of the people grew in variety and food supplies became secure, they could turn their attention to other cultural pursuits. A complex class system developed with workers performing the menial tasks thus allowing others to focus their efforts on art and science. The people learned to produce pottery that they used for household purposes; they dug pits to store food. Mathematics and astronomy grew out of the need to keep track of the festivals, and cities developed for efficient collection and distribution of goods, for ceremonial purposes, and for governing the regions that surrounded the cities.

As we look at the regions that produced social and technological complexity, we see patterns of (1) mild climates, (2) plentiful resources that then allow (3) cooperation, and (4) specialization. We can now make the following generalization:

The way people provide for their survival exerts an important influence on their social and political organization.

Where the climate was harsh and resources were scarce, people spent most of their time working merely to survive. Few people could be supported by the available resources and living was very basic and simple. Technology was limited and the social organization was restricted to the family or clan. Usually, the harsher the environment, the simpler the ways of life, and the greater the need for each person to be responsible for his or her survival. As a result, these simple cultures tended to be more democratic and less hierarchical in organization than the more complex ones.

Mild climates and plentiful resources characterized the complex cultures. Cooperation and specialization depended upon an abundance and surplus of food, for cooperation and specialization require that people have first met their basic needs for food, clothing, and shelter. Large-scale projects, whether positive and constructive such as irrigation canals, elaborate temples or burial mounds, or negative and destructive projects such as warfare, demanded cooperation. Specialization was necessary to refine art and technology.

The complex cultures tended to be affluent, and the level of differentiation in social class and the distribution of wealth was far greater among these people than in the simpler cultures.

Certainly, we can see the significant relationship between *where* a culture developed and the *type of culture* it became. There is a close relationship between the physical realities of environment and the development of a particular culture. The degree of sophistication and complexity of a particular Native American culture is closely related to the physical environment in which it developed.

Finally, in considering the importance of the physical environment and natural resources in the development of the physical culture, metaphysical beliefs and values of Native American peoples, classroom lesson plans should move beyond tipis, buffalo skins, corn pudding, sign language, and powwows to explore this important and sustaining relationship.

References

Baylor, B. *And It is Still That Way.* Santa Fe, N. Mex.: Trails West Publishing, 1988.

Baylor, B. *The Desert is Theirs.* New York: Macmillan, 1975.

Cornplanter, J. J. *Legends of the Longhouse.* Ontario, Canada: Iroqrafts Indian Publications, 1986.

Evers, L. *Between Sacred Mountains.* Tucson, Ariz.: Sun Tracks and the University of Arizona Press, 1986.

George, J.C. *Julie of the Wolves.* New York: Harper & Row, 1972.

Goble, P. *The Gift of the Sacred Dog.* New York: Bradbury Press, 1980.

Kopper, P. *The Smithsonian Book of North American Indians Before the Coming of the Europeans.* New York: Smithsonian Books, 1986.

McLuhan, T. C. *Touch the Earth*. New York: Simon & Schuster, 1971.

Morgan, W., ed. *Navajo Coyote Tales*. Santa Fe, N. Mex.: Ancient City Press, 1988.

Waldman, C. *Atlas of the North American Indian*. New York: Facts on File, 1985.

Wolfson, E. *From Abenaki to Zuni*. New York: Walker, 1988.

Lesson Plans

Grade Level: Intermediate

Basic Concepts: Environment and resources

Organizing Generalization: People use natural resources to meet their basic needs of food, clothing, and shelter.

Culture Area: *Any* of the Nine Regions

Time Period: Pre-European Contact

Background: You can adapt this general lesson plan to any locale or use it to compare and contrast cultural regions. Students will first study the physical environment and natural resources of one or more regions. Then they will be asked to hypothesize how the people of that area might have used what was available to them to meet their basic needs. There are "right" answers such as the *hogan* of the Navajo people of the *Southwest*. However, there are other reasonable choices. Students should be expected to give logical explanations for their selections. This is a good time to discuss culture, and the various choices people have made and continue to make to solve problems of survival. Native Americans demonstrated much creativity and ingenuity in adapting to their environment. Throughout this lesson, teachers will have to teach or review map and research skills.

Objectives:

Knowledge (Content)

Students will:

1. make a map of one region, including land forms and water bodies. Maps should indicate longitude and latitude and include a key;

2. make a physical map of the region that indicates different landforms and their elevation;

3. graph (a) average monthly rainfall, (b) average high and low temperatures, and (c) length of growing season; and

4. report on natural resources of the region, including vegetation, animals, and natural sources of food.

Skills

Students will:

1. hypothesize how people used the physical environment and natural resources to meet their basic needs;

2. use reasoned arguments to support their choices;

3. use reference materials for initial research and to verify their choices; and

4. work in cooperative groups.

Values (Organic)

Students will:

Appreciate the ingenuity and creativity of Native Americans.

Activities:

1. Initiate this lesson with a focused discussion of a hypothetical area (see below). Generate discussion as to how

people might live in this area. Guide students to think of the constraints and possibilities afforded by the physical environment and the resources. Some information is not available in this hypothetical area map. What kinds of information would students need in order to decide how people would meet their basic needs?

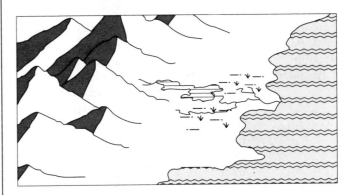

2. Divide students into cooperative groups for research and mapping activities (students may have the same or different regions to research). Many teachers will need to prepare research outlines for or with students.

3. Students will display completed maps and research results. Class will discuss maps and determine if they have enough information.

4. In groups of 2-4, students will use cards they prepare and label with the variety of foods, shelters, tools, and arts as a guide to decide how people might have used the environment in their study to meet their needs. They will present a final report on their selections to the class. Discussion of their selections should also include why some items were not selected as logical.

EXTENSIONS

1. Have works of fiction about Native Americans such as *Julie of the Wolves*, by Jean C. George (1972) available for students. There are many appropriate books that deal with survival.

2. A trip to a museum that focuses on early artifacts would be useful.

Evaluation:

It is suggested that teachers develop check lists of desired levels of the following competencies for use during and after the activity:

1. cooperative learning

2. map skills

3. research skills

4. critical thinking skills

5. reporting skills.

Materials and Resources:

The teacher or students will need to prepare laminated cards or large charts which have pictures of such items as:

Shelter	Food	Tools/Art
hogan	fish	birch bark canoes
longhouse	deer	fish nets
hide tipi	turkeys	baskets
pueblo	squash	clay pots
igloo	corn	travois
bark wigwam	beans	ivory needles
platform house	rabbits	hide shields
wickiup	moose	totem poles
earthen lodge	nuts and berries	quill work
	buffalo	digging sticks
	squirrel	bone tools (buffalo)
	caribou	short bows for hunting
	pumpkin	long bows
	dried meat	snares
	insects	looms
	roots	tanning equipment

George, J. C. *Julie of the Wolves.* New York: Harper & Row, 1972.

Waldman, C. *Atlas of the North American Indian.* New York: Facts on File, 1985.

Wolfson, E. *From Abenaki to Zuni.* New York: Walker, 1988.

Grade Level: Primary

Basic Concepts: Culture, environment, resources

Organizing Generalization: People develop stories about why things in the environment are the way they are. They tell these stories to their children and grandchildren to teach them about the world around them and the way their people live.

Culture Area: Southwest

Time Period: Pre-European Contact to the present

Background: During the winter, Navajo people spent many long hours in their hogans with their families. During this time, they told stories for instruction and entertainment. Long before the written word recorded the history and customs of traditional cultures, these stories told the meaning of life, why the world is as it is, and how to live in a proper way. Parents and grandparents spent many long hours telling and retelling the stories to teach their children about their way of life and their understanding of the world. This was their school. The teacher should help the students understand that the characters in the legends were often the animals in the surrounding environment and the stories all reflect the environment in which the children lived.

Objectives:

Knowledge (Content)

Students will:

1. name at least three animals that live in the desert;

2. describe, in their own words, what a desert is like (few trees—little water—dry-hot during summer days and cool at night—cold with occasional snow in the winter—large open spaces—few people and so on);

3. draw a desert picture with a hogan; and

4. experience the oral tradition process.

Skills

Students will:

1. retell a short story; and

2. identify the meaning or lesson in a story.

Values (Organic)

Students will:

1. begin to understand that the environment influences the way of life and culture of a people; and

2. understand how children learned about their way of life from stories and legends.

Activities:

1. Show a film, video, or filmstrip that depicts the desert or read *The Desert Is Theirs* (Baylor 1975). Take time to discuss and learn about desert animals.

2. Discuss the people who live in the desert, including the Navajo. Plenty of pictures should be available of the desert, desert animals, and the hogan.

3. Read a story from *Navajo Coyote Tales* (Morgan 1988) or *And It Is Still That Way* (Baylor 1988).

4. Discuss how families would tell stories to children during the long winter nights and how these stories were fun to hear and had lessons for the children. Continue to read the legends asking students to identify the lessons in the stories. Be sure to stress the oral tradition—the stories were not written down in books, but were remembered from generation to generation. The legends in *And it is Still That Way* (Baylor 1988) were written by Arizona children from their memories.

5. Read some of the stories several times so that children can tell them to each other.

6. Encourage students to think of stories that have meanings or lessons that their parents or grandparents have told them.

EXTENSIONS

1. Share legends of other Indian cultures.

2. Write a legend, using contemporary characters.

3. Invite a storyteller to class to tell stories.

Evaluation:

In their own words, children should be able to tell how legends and stories help children learn and that throughout the world many stories are remembered and told over and over again.

Materials and Resources:

Baylor, B. *And It Is Still That Way.* Santa Fe, N.Mex.: Trails West Publishing, 1988.

Arizona Indian children wrote these stories in school. Children will understand the language.

Baylor, B. *The Desert Is Theirs.* New York: Macmillan, 1975.

Cornplanter, J.J. *Legends of the Longhouse.* Ontario, Canada: Iroqrafts Indian Publications, 1986.

These stories are interesting background for the teacher but would need to be modified and retold orally for classroom use.

Goble, P. *The Gift of the Sacred Dog.* New York: Bradbury Press, 1980.

Morgan, W., ed. *Navajo Coyote Tales.* Santa Fe, N.Mex.: Ancient City Press, 1988.

This book is written in simplified English so that beginning readers can read it. Many others legends can be read to the students.

Grade Level: Secondary

Basic Concepts: Environment and resources

Organizing Generalization: The use of the earth's non-renewable resources has both long-term and short-term effects on our quality of life.

Cultural Area: Southwest

Time Period: Contemporary

Background: One of the challenges that all Americans face is the appropriate use of non-renewable resources. We all must make environmental decisions related to convenience versus conservation. It is important for individuals and groups to examine both long-term effects and short-term benefits of these decisions. The Navajo Nation faces particularly difficult environmental, economic, and cultural challenges related to the use of their non-renewable resources. Large stores of coal, oil, gas, and uranium are found underneath tribal lands. Mining these resources has political, economic, cultural, and moral implications. The ideas explored in this particular lesson or unit plan will assist students in understanding some of the problems faced by Navajo people and will engage them in learning the skills necessary to solving global environmental concerns.

Objectives:

Knowledge: (Content)

Students will:

1. summarize the history of Peabody Coal Company and their mining operations on Black Mesa; and

2. state the positive benefits and negative aspects of this mining operation for the Navajo people.

Skills:

Students will:

1. use research skills;

2. practice cooperative skills in gathering information;

3. detect perspective in the differing accounts of the mining operations;

4. recognize propaganda and self-serving statements and actions; and

5. hypothesize as to the long-term effects of decisions regarding the mining operations.

Values. (Organic)

Students will:

1. recognize that every action has a reaction, and that environmental decisions of today will affect the quality of life tomorrow;

2. appreciate the dilemma facing the Navajo who are experiencing overcrowding and high rates of unemployment on reservation lands; and

3. develop interest in global environmental issues.

Activities:

1. The questions that will guide this study are posed by Navajo people in the book *Between Sacred Mountains* edited by Larry Evers (1982). These questions are related to the mining of non-renewable resources on the reservation (see also Decision Tree at end of this lesson):

   a. Can we satisfy our needs in ways other than mining?

   b. What will happen if we do not agree to sign the agreement with Peabody Coal (to mine the resources)?

   c. Who will benefit?

   d. Who will lose?

   e. How much land will we lose and whose land will it be?

   f. How much money does the tribe need?

   g. Why does the tribe need money?

   h. Are there any benefits from the mining operation other than money?

   i. What new ideas and ways of life do we wish to encourage?

   j. Will old ideas and ways of life be strengthened or weakened?

   k. Are we willing to take responsibility for what happens?

2. Group students into research teams. Each team should have a particular topic to investigate. Suggested topical themes include: historical, cultural, political, environmental, economic, and ethical issues. The questions stated above should guide the study of each topic.

3. After sharing the results of their research, students will compile answers to the basic questions that guided this study. Depending on the depth of the study, the abilities of the students, and the length of time available, this

could be done as individual summary reports or by discussion with the entire class.

EXTENSIONS

1. Apply the same questions to important local or global environmental issues.

2. Write letters expressing opinions on the contracts with Peabody Coal to governmental, tribal, or Peabody leaders.

Evaluation:

Using the information gathered about the mining operations of Peabody Coal on the Navajo Reservation, students will answer the suggested questions.

Materials and Resources:

Evers, L. *Between Sacred Mountains*. Tucson: Sun Tracks and the University of Arizona Press, 1986.

This excellent book presents information from a Navajo perspective. The teacher is encouraged to use a wide variety of resources.

Information from the mining company's perspective may be obtained by writing:

Peabody Coal Company
P.O. Box 606
Kayenta, AZ 86033

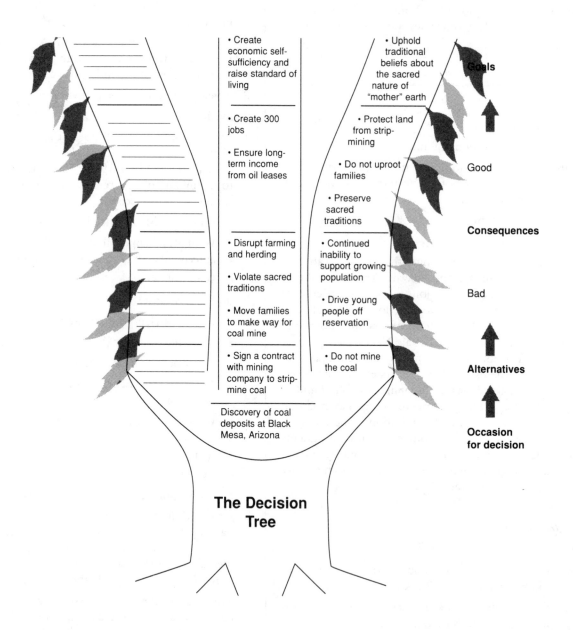

The Decision Tree

- Create economic self-sufficiency and raise standard of living
- Create 300 jobs
- Ensure long-term income from oil leases

- Disrupt farming and herding
- Violate sacred traditions
- Move families to make way for coal mine

- Sign a contract with mining company to strip-mine coal

- Uphold traditional beliefs about the sacred nature of "mother" earth
- Protect land from strip-mining
- Do not uproot families
- Preserve sacred traditions

- Continued inability to support growing population
- Drive young people off reservation

- Do not mine the coal

Discovery of coal deposits at Black Mesa, Arizona

Goals
Good
Consequences
Bad
Alternatives
Occasion for decision

Adapted from a device developed by Roger LaRaus and Richard C. Remy. Used with permission.

CHAPTER THREE
CULTURE AND DIVERSITY

You have noticed that everything that an Indian does is in a circle, and that is because the Power of the World always works in circles, and everything tries to be round. In the old days when we were a strong and happy people, all our power came to us from the sacred hoop of the nation and so long as the hoop was unbroken, the people flourished. The flowering tree was the living center of the hoop, and the circle of the four quarters nourished it. The east gave peace and light, the south gave warmth, the west gave rain, and the north with its cold and mighty wind gave strength and endurance. This knowledge came to us from the outer world with our religion. Everything the Power of the World does is done in a circle. The sky is round, and I have heard that the earth is round like a ball, and so are the stars. The wind, in its greatest power, whirls. Birds make their nests in circles, for theirs is the same religion as ours. The sun comes forth and goes down again in a circle. The moon does the same, and both are round. Even the seasons form a great circle in their changing, and always come back again to where they were. The life of a man is a circle from childhood to childhood, and so it is in everything where power moves. Our teepees were round like the nests of birds, and these were always set in a circle, the nation's hoop, a nest of many nests, where the Great Spirit meant for us to hatch our children.

—Black Elk (Neihardt 1973)

CULTURE AND DIVERSITY

Culture: The behavior patterns, belief systems, artifacts, and other human-made components of a society, including the foods that people eat, the tools they use, their clothing, myths, religion, and language. Culture consists of those elements that humans use to adjust or adapt to their physical and social environment.

Diversity: The condition of being different or having differences.

The cultures of Native Americans have attracted the attention of all races of people, both young and old alike. They marvel at ancient decorative art on pottery and cave walls, woven products such as baskets and clothing, and knowledge of architecture, astrology, and astronomy. Some study the spiritual wisdom of Native religion and life, seeking their own peace and harmony. Others seek healing knowledge and plant properties.

Although this type of interest and study is common, it does not provide a valid or complete view of the life and history of the Native American people. Slices of time and place, considered alone like tiny "factlets," rather than parts of a whole do not provide students enough information to develop useful concepts and social science principles. This chapter will provide an overview of the concepts of culture and diversity throughout Native American communities.

Native American people are creative and the cultures in the nine geographic regions are very different from each other in language, dress, food, ceremonies, and rituals.

James Banks (1977) states that culture is a people's solution to the problem of survival. Viewed in this way, culture begins with the ways people use or adapt the surrounding physical environment and the available natural resources to meet their basic survival needs and grows to encompass the many ways they live out their daily lives.

In studying the life of humans on this planet, scholars have identified similarities so deep and broad as to suggest possible relationships between people from varying continents. At the same time, they have discovered staggering variations and contrasts between cultures and ways of life of people who live within a short distance of each other. These patterns, for the most part, can be attributed to the specific natural resources available to the people and how they used them to meet their basics needs of survival including food, clothing, and shelter.

The cultures of the native inhabitants of North America developed simultaneously and yet independently of outside cultures and their influences for approximately 12,000-40,000 years (Kopper 1986). These Native American cultures evolved through time with distinct languages, social customs, clothing, foods, means of shelter, tools, and histo-ries. During the Pre-European Contact Period, it is estimated that they spoke more than 500 languages. Upon contact, over 200 languages were recorded. These languages were classified into 73 language families and 8 distinct groups. Two different tribes, in two very diverse physical environments, illustrate this diversity and social science generalization well.

The **Seneca**, members of the Iroquois Confederacy of the **Northeast Region**, constructed their homes out of log poles with bark thatch shingles for walls and the roof. They left a hole in the roof for light and smoke. The house was shaped like a rectangle and was called a longhouse. They employed the same type of architecture for dwellings as well as meeting places and ceremonial lodges. The Seneca fashioned poles and bark shingles from oak, elm, spruce, or white cedar, all natural to their environment. Some longhouses were 25 feet (7.62 meters) long and used for dwellings for a large number of people, whereas others were 200 feet (60.96 meters) long and housed the Great Council of the Confederacy.

Corn constituted the main staple of the Seneca diet. The people were skilled agriculturalists, raising not only corn, but beans, squash, and pumpkins. They hunted deer and small game animals and collected berries and other wild fruits and vegetables. They made clothing from the skins of the animals they killed. They met their needs through the creative use of the natural resources of their physical environment.

In contrast to the Seneca, the **Navajo** of the **Southwest Region** used their environment to meet their shelter needs by constructing hogans out of available pine and mud plaster. Primitive hogans were conical, whereas modern hogans are six-sided. The hogan is always built with the opening in the east, toward the sunrise. Hogans have a central roof opening for allowing smoke to escape and light to enter. They often build simple shelters with brush roofs or shade houses near the hogan for cooking and shelter during the intense hours of desert heat.

Traditional tribal history suggests that the Navajo can trace their ancestry in the Southwest Region as far as they can trace it through their oral history and legends. Scientific evidence, however, suggests that they came south to their present home in the 1400s. Facts such as the Navajo language is of the Athapascan family, primarily found in Alaska and Canada, support this theory. When the Navajo arrived in the Southwest, they found the Pueblo people cultivating fields of corn, beans, and pumpkins. The Pueblo people wove cloth out of cotton, fashioned baskets out of weeds, and made pottery, turquoise beads, and tools to cultivate the soil. At the time of contact, the Navajo were wanderers who hunted game and gathered berries. Immediately, they began to learn from the Pueblo people and began to develop their rich heritage of weaving. Soon they gained sheep from the Spaniards and began raising herds for food and clothing. In these ways, they used their southwestern desert environment to meet their basic needs.

Cultural similarities exist between groups of Native American people in the past and present. These similarities are manifested in the spiritual beliefs of Native Americans and provide the foundation for their way of life.

Culture also has meaning beyond how people meet their needs and wants for survival. Culture also includes shared meanings, experiences, and understandings that are passed from one generation to another. The guiding spiritual or metaphysical beliefs of Native Americans are probably more important to understand than the observable phenomena of tools, dwelling, clothing, food, laws, and tribal government.

Although the previous examples illustrate the diverse ways that native peoples have used the environment to meet their survival needs, it is also true that powerful similarities exist of shared meanings, beliefs, and values. A closer look at Native cultures will reveal common threads that transcend the distinctive characteristics of the physical environment or region.

Alfonso Ortiz (Morris 1983) uses the term *worldview*, explaining that worldview "provides people with a distinctive set of values, an identity, a feeling of 'rootedness,' of belonging to a time and a place, and a felt sense of continuity with a tradition that transcends the experience of a single lifetime, a tradition that may be said to transcend even time." It is this worldview that creates the sense of "Indianness," the similarity that supersedes the differences made necessary by physical environment.

Scholars have identified the following questions that provide indicators of worldviews (Levin and Bates 1985).

- What is the nature of **time**—is it oriented toward the past, present, or future?

- What is the nature of humankind's **relationship to the physical world**—does it emphasize mastery over, harmony with, or subjugation to the environment?

- What is the nature of **activity**—is it becoming (spiritual), or doing (achievement)?

- What is the nature of **human relationships**—are they hierarchical, collective, or individualistic?

- What is **human nature**—is it good, bad, or neutral?

It is useful to apply the concept of the ecosystem to examine the similarities between groups of Native American people in the past and continuing to the present. An ecosystem is a community of animals and plants and the natural environment in which they live. In their natural or primal form, balanced ecosystems are self-perpetuating. They provide an environment where, if all participating elements are functioning, they contribute to the health, wellness and perpetuation of the whole system and each member.

The varying landscapes of North America provides for a wide variety of local ecosystems. Native inhabitants lived for thousands of years, playing a contributing role in the balance and maintenance of their system. They believed that each member of the ecosystem was there for a purpose. This primary philosophy, along with several other identifiable universal beliefs, guided the way that individual members of the group lived their lives and the way that the entire culture evolved over time.

These concepts of worldview and ecosystem are evident today in the lifestyle and culture of the Native American. They have been manifested throughout time in varying form.

- Native Americans believe in the interdependence of all creations. They believe that all things (both living and inanimate) are created for a purpose in the natural cycle of the world. Human beings share this purpose. Interdependence was an integral part of traditional life and helped maintain the natural balance of the environment. The Lakota People, who reside in the **Plains Region,** conclude their prayers with the words Mitakuye Oyasin. This means "All my relations" or "We are all related." When ending a prayer with these words, the person expresses that the one praying is including a prayer for all creations. In this way the people are constantly reminded of their role in the whole of life and their responsibility to all creations.

- Native Americans believe in an ultimate Creator. Some people refer to this Creator as the Giver of Breath, whereas others use the terms Grandfather, Great Spirit, All Spirit, or Great Mystery. They believe that the Creator is everywhere and can hear, see, and knows all, and address the Creator in most prayers with great reverence.

- Religion for Native Americans is not separated from daily existence. It is intertwined into the act of life. Art is also integrated into the whole of life. A woman in times past would create an earthen pot to carry and store water. She would paint a symbol on the outside to represent water or the abundance of it. She believed that if she was aware of water and the role that it played in her life, and aware of the natural laws, water would be plentiful. In this way, her art and religion were embodied in her daily life.

- Language of Native people of North America developed through need and function. Although vast differences exist among the languages, the function and metaphysical meaning of language is similar. The words have power and are sacred. Words are not spoken for the sake of talking, but to impart a message. Speech initiates from the center of the body where the heart and breath also abide. Speaking involves an audible bond between humans and all creations.

- Native Americans believe in a world beyond the physical world. Some call it the spirit world or the world of unseen powers. One world is not without the other and both worlds are real.

• People, as well as all creations, are made of body and spirit. Native prayers, ceremonies, and songs call upon the spirits of the creations to come to their aid. They believe that all creations of Grandfather are of the physical and spirit world.

These basic premises pervaded the lives of early Native Americans. They guided the way that the people used the natural resources to meet their needs. Therefore, even though the resources varied in the different geographic regions, Native Americans throughout all regions shared their respect for the land and the other inhabitants of this world. It becomes evident why they could live for so long without disturbing the natural balance as other civilizations of the world have been known to do.

Native Americans throughout time have taught their children the ways of their culture and thus ensured the perpetuation of the culture.

Each cultural group transmits the essential body of knowledge regarding its people to the new generations. By doing so, they help preserve their sacred traditions and keys to survival and they perpetuate their culture. Like other cultural traits, the methods used to share the knowledge is directly linked to the essential beliefs of the culture.

Three primary methods of educating new generations found among Native Americans are (1) the use of oral traditions, (2) the technique of observation, and (3) participation and personal experience. All three are interwoven into everyday life.

The oral tradition, use of myths, stories, legends, and song is common throughout North America. In some tribes, storytelling is done only in winter, whereas in others there is no seasonal link. Legends were used to pass on specific knowledge about how the people handled natural calamities, illness, significant life passages, and other lifetime events. Although a humorous trickster was often woven into the fabric of the legend, its purpose was more than humor. There was and always is a meaning or purpose for the legend. Today, many of these legends are still being told, word for word, just as the Old Ones told them. Songs are sung at ceremonials, in healing ceremonies, social gatherings, and life passages. They are also sung today as they were in the past. Elders of the past used the legends to teach their children how to live and parents and teachers of today use them in the same way.

Observation of family and community members provides the broadest method of communicating survival techniques. Children began at a very young age to observe the actions of their elders. When they were ready, they were taken by the appropriate family members and kept with them while they performed tasks associated with survival and everyday life. The children learned by close observation and from imitating the activities and behaviors of others.

Finally, Native American children were taught through the use of personal experience. This is generally associated

with vision quests and other ceremonies to help individuals gain strength and power to deal with daily life. Children participated in these rites when it was appropriate by virtue of age, gender, and experience. Children were never separated from the community or family for the purpose of education. Education was living with the community and family.

It is easy to see how government-ordered disruption of the family and the imposition of a different kind of education, a new language, and "foreign" ways of learning have affected the perpetuation of living native cultures. This disruption, a result of governmental policies of forced assimilation, has had lasting, perhaps irreversible effects on Native American peoples and their cultures.

The forced separation of children from their families created a new generation of Indians that functioned only marginally in the dominant society and only marginally in their own cultures. One long-lasting effect of this marginality has been that this generation, frequently deprived of strong cultural role models and with weakened pride and self-confidence, has a diminished sense of family membership. As a consequence, they have difficulty creating strong, enduring families and often demonstrate ineffective parenting skills. Perpetuation of the culture could be in jeopardy, at least through traditional methods.

Native Americans are striving to maintain and perpetuate their Indian cultures by several new methods. One strategy has been the creation of the urban Indian Center. Indian people migrate to the city from many tribes throughout the country. Indian Centers are located in most highly urbanized areas and serve as "home" to many Indians in this new environment. These centers provide support, job counseling, social gatherings, programs for children, young people, and the elderly, and social service and substance-abuse programs for new arrivals.

Another phenomena, Pan-Indianism, has developed as a result of a growing common consciousness among Native Americans as an ethnic group. Pan-Indianism is defined as "the sharing of common interests by Indians of many tribes in certain dances, ceremonials, and music of the Plains and Oklahoma tribes" (Spicer 1983). The powwows that are held across the country, particularly in the summer months, enable Indians from cities and reservations to share costumes, dances, foods, and songs. In a sense, powwows are ceremonies of sharing and a celebration of a common cultural heritage. This is another way in which contemporary Native Americans keep their cultures and sense of "Indianness" alive for their children.

Finally, Native cultures are perpetuated by formal educational efforts. Some schools, such as Navajo Community College in Tsaile, Arizona, Haskell Indian Junior College in Lawrence, Kansas, and the Santa Fe, New Mexico, Indian Art School, serve primarily to provide quality, culturally-sensitive educational programs for Native American students. They also bring together young people from a variety of tribes resulting in inter-tribal marriages and a growing sense of Pan-Indianism. Schools, like Rough Rock Community School on the Navajo Reservation in Arizona, that have contracted with the Bureau of Indian Affairs (B.I.A.) for unique programs also focus on tribal language, history, and culture. B.I.A. schools have now become more sensitive to the importance of culture than they were in the past. There is considerable emphasis on hiring Native American personnel in B.I.A. schools and dormitories and on creating both competency and self-respect in Indian youth.

A wealth of Native American cultures was disrupted, and in all too many cases destroyed, by the coming of Europeans to the Western Hemisphere. Yet, from the torn and stained fabric of Indian-white affairs, emerged a strong thread, a "spirit line" as it were, running to the present day—the will and ability of American Indian people to survive; changed, but with traditions intact. No less vital and significant than previous ones, new fabrics of Indian life have been strongly woven in the mid-twentieth century. (Herold 1978, 2)

References

Anderson, J. *The First Thanksgiving Feast*. New York: Clarion, 1984.

Ball, W. W. R. *Fun With String Games*. New York: Clarion, 1984.

Banks, J.A., with A. A. Cleft, Jr. *Teaching Strategies for the Social Studies*. Reading, Mass.: Addison-Wesley, 1977.

Cohen, H., and T. Coffin, eds. *The Folklore of American Holidays*. Detroit, Mich.: Gale Research Company, 1987.

Gryski, C. *Cat's Cradle, Owl's Eyes: A Book of String Games*. New York: Morrow, 1983.

Gryski, C. *Many Stars and More String Games*. New York: Morrow, 1985.

Gryski, C. *Super String Games*. New York: Morrow, 1987.

Hammerschlag, C. *The Dancing Healer*. New York: Harper & Row, 1988.

Herold, J. *The Urban Indian Experience: A Denver Portrait*. Denver, Colo.: Denver Museum of Natural History, 1978.

Kessel, J.K. *Squanto and the First Thanksgiving*. Minneapolis, Minn.: Carolrhoda Books, 1983.

Kluckholn, B., and D. Leighton. *The Navajo*. Cambridge, Mass.: Harvard University Press, 1974.

Kopper, P. *The Smithsonian Book of North American Indians Before the Coming of the Europeans*. New York: Smithsonian Books, 1986.

Levin, J., and J. L. Bates. *Starting Sociology*. New York: Harper & Row, 1985.

Neihardt, J.G. *Black Elk Speaks*. New York: Pocket Books, 1973.

Ortiz, A. "Introduction: Cultural Values and Leadership Development." In J. Morris. *Ohoyo Training Manual—Leadership; Self-Help, American Indian—Alaska Native Women*. Wichita Falls, Tex.: Ohoyo Resource Center, 1983.

Ramsey, P. G. "Beyond 'Ten Little Indians' and Turkeys." *Young Children* (September 1979): 28-51.

Seawall, M. *The Pilgrims of Plimoth*. New York: Atheneum, 1986.

Spicer, E. H. *A Short History of the Indians of the United States*. Malabar, Fla.: Robert E. Krieger, 1983.

Williamson, D., and L. Railsback. *Cooking With Spirit: North American Indian Food and Fact*. Bend, Ore.: Maverick Publications, 1987.

Lesson Plans

Grade Level: Secondary

Basic Concepts: Culture, diversity, and ethnocentrism.

Organizing Generalization: Situations, actions, and events of any cultural group are interpreted through the cultural perspective of the observer.

Culture Area: Southwest

Time Period: Contemporary

Background: In order for students to study and understand other cultures, it is important for them to understand that any situation, action, or event has only contextual meaning. Interpretation of events from an uninformed or ethnocentric point of view can provide only a distorted meaning. Judgments made from ethnocentric perspectives are often invalid and can lead to serious misunderstanding between cultures and the formation of superficial stereotypes.

Objectives:

Knowledge (Content)

Students will:

1. demonstrate basic understanding of the generalization by giving a concrete example; and

2. state at least three problems that could occur between cultures when cultural perspectives are not considered when interpreting the behaviors of another cultural group.

Skills

Students will:

1. give a factual, descriptive account of an event;

2. hypothesize the values of a people that are demonstrated in an event; and

3. distinguish between a descriptive and an interpretative account of an event.

Values (Organic)

Students will:

1. understand that cultural differences are often interpreted as negative when viewed from an ethnocentric perspective; and

2. begin to seek to understand another's perspective before making a value judgment on their behavior(s).

Activities:

1. Prepare a worksheet for each student. Divide the class into partners, giving each team two worksheets.

2. Each team will read the cultural accounts and complete a worksheet for each account.

3. After sharing some of the worksheet responses of each group the class will discuss the following question: What, if any, is the value of this exercise?

4. Each student will submit an "I learned…" statement.

EXTENSIONS

1. Some students might want to discuss how typical teen behavior appears to teachers and parents, and how it might be misunderstood.

2. Investigate or arrange an actual demonstration of Navajo sand painting.

3. Extra credit could be awarded for research into Native American traditional methods of healing.

4. Those students with strong reading skills would enjoy reading *The Dancing Healer* (Hammerschlag 1988).

Evaluation:

The "I learned" statements will indicate if students have an understanding of the generalization.

Materials and Resources:

Hammerschlag, C. *The Dancing Healer*. New York: Harper & Row, 1988.

CULTURAL ACCOUNT OF AN AMERICAN CEREMONY[*]

One important ceremony in the American culture involves a seasonal ceremony involving two religious factions. The religious contests are held during the colder months in specially constructed ceremonial grounds surrounded by seats for people who, although not practitioners of the religion, seem not to be merely observers either. It is not clear what stake they have in the proceedings, unless it is to support, encourage, or possibly to record or learn a religion lesson from the participants of the ceremony. It appears not to be a historical pageant, for the outcome of the contest varies.

The participants themselves are dressed from head to foot in ceremonial garb especially designed to protect them during the ceremony. All of the representatives are male and are dressed alike except for color. The participants represent two distinct sects with the symbols that represent their deity or sect on their headgear.

Several other men are dressed in black and white clothing without protection. Their function in the ceremony seems to be that of high priests, since a shrill noise from them has the power to halt the ceremony while they make dramatic gestures that seem to be part of the ritual and have meaning to the participants and the observers. On occasion, humans dressed as animals dance about the arena, somewhat similar to kachinas. Usually there are several other male and female participants dressed in the same colors, but performing the function of exciting the observers, rather than participating directly in the ceremony.

The ceremonial arena itself has been decorated with religious markings and writings that seem to designate the significance of certain parts of the field.

The two areas at each end of the arena appear to be the holiest locations and the object of the contest seems to be to reach this holy sanctuary, since the response from the participants and the spectators is the most energetic when one of these areas has been entered, especially when the religious representative possesses an odd-shaped oblong object that is pointed at each end. This object seems to hold great religious significance to both sides and their supporters in the surrounding seats. The possession of this sacred object appears to be one of the objectives of the contest.

Although the participants in each contest change from time to time, the activities of the ceremony involve lining up facing each other and, at some mysterious signal, each representative in the arena struggles with or tries to escape his opposite, or will sometimes try to catch and harm the possessor of the oblong icon. Each group meets together occasionally on the field to pray, but it is unclear whether these prayers are for strength, victory, or just courage for the next encounter.

Brute strength and running speed seem to be highly prized abilities in this religious sect. It appears to be a very common religion in America.

CULTURAL ACCOUNT OF A NATIVE AMERICAN CEREMONY*

One important ceremony among Navajo People involves a group of people, perhaps a family, and a leader. The leader is always male. The leader consults frequently with the group before the ceremony begins. The ceremony is held in or around the home which is a six-sided log structure with one room.

The most important part of the ceremony consists of the leader making highly stylized pictures or paintings, in somewhat the fashion of medieval glass painting. The paints are made from charcoal and minerals that have been ground into a fine sand which is then used in dry form. It is difficult to determine the symbolism of the figures in the paintings because the paintings will differ from occasion to occasion. Over five hundred different paintings have been recorded.

Some of these paintings are miniatures, only a foot or two in diameter. Others are so large, twenty feet or more in diameter that they can be made only in specially constructed homes. The small ones can be made by two or three people in less than an hour. The largest ones require the work of fifteen men during most of a day. In some ceremonies only a single painting is made, but in others as many as four paintings are made on as many as nine successive days.

Most of the paintings are created in the home, but some are made out-of-doors. Also most of them are made in the daytime, but a few are created after dark. Before the leader begins to create the painting, charcoal and minerals are prepared and placed in bark receptacles. Clean light-colored wind-blown sand is carried into the home and spread over the floor in an even layer from one to three inches thick.

Sometimes the background is a buckskin. The leader and his assistants kneel or sit on the background to create the design. Colors vary, but the four principal hues—white, blue, yellow, and black—are always present.

Most of the color is laid on with the right hand of the leader, who holds the coloring matter against his palm with his closed fingers and lets it trickle out through the aperture between the thumb and flexed index finger. Some parts of the picture are measured by palms and spans; others are drawn freely. Straight lines of any length are made by snapping a cotton string held by two persons. The picture is smoothed off at intervals with a wooden stick. Errors are not rubbed out but covered over with the neutral shade of the background. The painters work from the center out, and from left to right. Frequently a stylized rainbow surrounds the picture on all sides but the east. The patterns seem to be in the memory of the leader.

When the painting has been completed, accompanied by songs and chants, a person from the group sits on it in a particular fashion. This person is given a mixture of herbs to drink. The leader works with this person for a time by touching and chanting. Most likely the ceremony honors or perhaps treats this particular person. Members of the group surround the painting and the seated person.

When this is finished and the person being "treated" goes outside, the painting is destroyed bit by bit in the order in which it was made. The sand is swept up and carried out to the north of the home. The rest of the group may walk in ceremonial fashion around the painting, treading where the figures have been.

The order and details of the ceremony appear to be important and mistakes by the leader seem to be considered quite serious, even dangerous by the group.

The ceremony is accompanied by unintelligible songs or chants by the leaders. Rattles are used by the leader as well as a stick that makes a groaning sound when whirled by the leader. Other paraphernalia used in the ceremony include aromatic substances burned like incense, natural objects like shells and stones, and mysterious "bundles."

CULTURAL ACCOUNTS OF AMERICAN CEREMONIES

1. What is being described?

2. What is factually correct about this description? How do you know?

3. What is wrong with this description? How do you know?

4. Has the writer ever talked to anyone who knows about this event?

5. Does this account tell very much about the culture of the participants? If so, what?

6. Does it tell very much about the culture of the writer? If so, what?

7. If the writer added more information to this account,

would it be more accurate? What information is needed?

8. Does the account need revision or change? If so, what?

9. If changes are needed, how could they be made?

10. How could the best description of this event be achieved?

* The originator of "A Cultural Account of an American Ceremony" is Eulala Pegram, member of the Creek Tribe, who is a teacher in Colorado Springs, Colorado. The material used in "A Cultural Account of a Native American Ceremony" was adapted from Kluckholn and Leighton (1974).

Grade Level: Primary

Basic Concepts: Culture and diversity

Organizing Generalization: Indian people had different ways of living in the past. Indian people lived differently in the past than they do in the present.

Culture Area: Northeast

Time Period: Post-European Contact—1840s or Contemporary

Background: This lesson provides an alternative strategy for teaching about Thanksgiving. Many typical Thanksgiving activities perpetuate stereotypes that dehumanize Native Americans. Commonly used songs ("Ten Little Indians"), activities (school Thanksgiving dinners), and costumes (Indian headdresses) are not accurate and are often considered offensive to Indian people. For example, the Wampanoag people, who lived where Plymouth Rock stands, and who probably participated in the first Thanksgiving, did not wear feather headdresses. Native Americans were tribally specific in the past and although they have changed in many ways, still maintain their diverse languages and culture in modern times. The following three questions should be asked when considering an activity for Thanksgiving in the classroom (Ramsey 1979).

1. Do the proposed activities in any way support or reinforce negative and dehumanizing images of Native Americans?

2. Do they imply or confirm historical misconceptions about the relationships between Europeans and Americans?

3. Are the experiences of all the people involved realistically represented?

This lesson is designed to teach about Thanksgiving and not reinforce negative stereotypes of Native Americans.

Objectives:

Knowledge (Content)

Students will:

1. identify how the Wampanoag people dressed at the first Thanksgiving;

2. recognize that different Indian tribes dressed differently in the past;

3. discuss how Indian people were different from each other in the past;

4. identify how Indian people are different now from how they were in the past;

5. discuss how Indian people might be similar to Indian people of the past; and

6. recognize stereotypes in contemporary portrayals of the first Thanksgiving.

Skills

Students will:

1. use observation skills in comparing and contrasting different clothing styles in the past and present, and between different cultural groups;

2. compare the dress of the Wampanoag with the dress of Plains Indian tribes during the the same time period;

3. compare the dress of the Wampanoag people with that of the Pilgrims; and

4. compare the dress of the Wampanoag at the first Thanksgiving with the dress of contemporary Indians.

Values (Organic)

Students will:

1. understand that Indian people, like all people, are diverse; and

2. appreciate cooperative efforts between Indians and Pilgrims.

Activities:

1. Read *The First Thanksgiving Feast* (Anderson 1984) to the students. Allow ample time for looking at the illustrations. Each of the books listed below presents different perspectives and several have language that will seem difficult for young children. Teachers may use the books as references and *tell* the story, using the illustrations.

2. Plan a Thanksgiving dinner to share at school. Part of the preparations should include discussion on how students can simulate the *real* first Thanksgiving with accurate costumes and foods. (Plimoth, featured in two books, is a living history museum in Plymouth, Massachusetts).

3. Lead a discussion on the following questions:

   a. Who attended the first Thanksgiving?

   b. What did the Pilgrims look like? What did they wear?

   c. What did the Indians look like? What did they wear?

   d. What did they eat at the first Thanksgiving?

   e. Did the Pilgrims and Indians speak the same language?

   f. How do you think they were alike? different?

   g. How did the Pilgrims and Indians share and help each other at the first Thanksgiving?

4. After observing the dress of the Wampanoags, discuss pictures of Plains Indian tribes (usually the stereotypical

Indian). Are they alike? different? Explain.

5. Introduce pictures of contemporary Native Americans in business suits, jeans, and so on. Are they alike? different? Explain.

EXTENSIONS

1. Students should also plan for authentic food (or close approximations) to be served at the dinner. This provides the opportunity to discuss how cultures change over time (clothing, food, occupations) and how some things remain constant (languages, ceremonies, values).

2. Planning for authenticity in food will provide an opportunity to discuss how Pilgrims and Indians used natural resources.

3. A Thanksgiving feast at school will provide many opportunities for students to work cooperatively and to share in the Indian tradition.

4. The prayer shown at the end of this activity, "The Thanksgivings," from the Seneca Green Corn Dance Ceremony could be adapted for choral reading.

Evaluation:

Students will be able to state the generalizations in their own words.

Materials and Resources:

Anderson, J. *The First Thanksgiving Feast*. New York: Clarion, 1984.

Cohen, H., and T. P. Coffin, eds. *The Folklore of American Holidays*. Detroit, Mich.: Gale Research Company, 1987.

Kessel, J.K. *Squanto and the First Thanksgiving*. Minneapolis, Minn.: Carolrhoda Books, 1983.

Seawall, M. *The Pilgrims of Plimoth*. New York: Atheneum, 1986.

Williamson, D., and L. Railsback. *Cooking with Spirit: North American Indian Food and Fact*. Bend, Ore.: Maverick Publications, 1987.

Pictures of Plains Indians in traditional dress.

Pictures of Indian people in contemporary dress.

A supply of Thanksgiving greeting cards, table decorations, or other Thanksgiving books that depict accurately or inaccurately the dress of historical and contemporary Indians.

"THE THANKSGIVINGS"

We who are here present thank the Great Spirit that we are here to praise Him.

We thank Him that He has created men and women, and ordered that these beings shall always be living to multiply the earth.

We thank Him for making the earth and giving these beings its products to live on.

We thank Him for the water that comes out of the earth and runs for our lands.

We thank Him for all the animals on the earth.

We thank Him for certain timbers that grow and have fluids coming from them (referring to the maple) for us all.

We thank Him for the branches of the trees that grow shadows for our shelter.

We thank Him for the beings that come from the west, the thunder and lightning that water the earth.

We thank Him for the light which we call our oldest brother, the sun that works for our good.

We thank Him for all the fruits that grow on the trees and vines.

We thank Him for his goodness in making the forests, and thank all its trees.

We thank Him for the darkness that gives us rest, and for the kind Being of the darkness that gives us light, the moon.

We thank Him for the bright spots in the skies that give us signs, the stars.

We give Him thanks for our supporters, who have charge of our harvests. (In the mythology of the Iroquois Indians there is a most beautiful conception of these "Our Supporters." They are three sisters of great beauty, who delight to dwell in the companionship of each other as the spiritual guardians of the corn, the beans, and the squash. These vegetables, the staple food of the red man, are supposed to be in the special care of the Great Spirit, who, in the growing season, sends these "supporters" to abide in the fields and protect them from the ravages of blight or frost. These guardians are clothed in the leaves of their respective plants, and, though invisible, are faithful and vigilant.)

We give thanks that the voice of the Great Spirit can still be heard through the words of Ga-ne-o-di-o (Handsome Lake).

We thank the Great Spirit that we have the privilege of this pleasant occasion.

We give thanks for the persons who can sing the Great Spirit's music, and hope they will be privileged to continue in his faith.

We thank the Great Spirit for all the persons who perform the ceremonies on this occasion.

From the "Great Feather Dance," one of the most imposing dances of the Iroquois, which is dedicated to the worship of the Great Spirit and part of the Seneca Green Corn Dance, in Cohen, H., and T. P. Coffin, eds. *The Folklore of American Holidays*. Detroit, Mich.: Gale Research Company, 1987, 342.

Grade Level: Intermediate

Basic Concepts: Culture and similarity

Organizing Generalizations: Although cultures are different in many ways, they are also alike in many ways.

Culture Area: General

Time Period: All periods

Background: Indian children, throughout North America, play string games. Anthropologists have discovered that these same games are played by children throughout the world. Camilla Gryski (1983) comments that "anthropologists used to be described as people with their pockets full of string." String games have different names in various cultures, but many of the figures are still the same. String games are fun and can be used to teach about culture and to reinforce map skills. String figures also tell something about the people who did them and the environment in which they lived, the beliefs they had about playing string games, what things were important to them, and what things made them laugh. James R. Murphy, a teacher in New York, is pioneering work in using string games to teach thinking skills and abstract mathematical skills and concepts (fig. 3.1).

Objectives:

Knowledge (Content)

Students will:

1. discuss how string games are used for recreation and how they are part of the oral tradition of Native American cultures;

2. recognize that string games are played throughout the world;

3. discuss why they believe string games are played by so many children throughout the world (including that they did not have libraries, television, radio, electric lights, automobiles or public transportation, and shopping malls); and

4. demonstrate how string games were used to tell stories about the culture.

Skills

Students will:

1. form one or more string figures;

2. locate on a map where designated string games are played; and

3. work with each other to learn some string figures.

Values (Organic)

Students will:

appreciate and enjoy games of simpler times.

Activities:

1. The books listed below contain very clear directions on how to make the strings and how to form the figures. The illustrations are excellent and each figure has a brief description of the cultures that use particular figures. Teachers will need to learn several figures in order to demonstrate them to the children. Select easy figures that have interesting stories and that are done in several parts of the world.

2. Large charts should be prepared with the basic steps for beginning to learn about string figures.

3. Provide a large map for students to locate countries where people also play string games.

4. Encourage students to work with each other to learn the figures.

EXTENSIONS

1. Students may want to investigate other Indian games or the games of early European settlers and learn to play them. Games give much insight into the physical environment and lifeways of a culture.

2. Read about how anthropologists coded the directions for string games. See *Fun with String Figures* (Ball 1971).

Evaluation:

Students will demonstrate to another class a variety of string games and tell about how they were used in diverse cultures. It would be useful for each student to teach a figure to another student and tell the story that accompanies the figure.

Figure 3.1

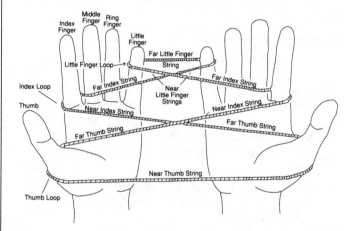

From *Cat's Cradle, Owl's Eyes: A Book of String Games*, by Carmilla Gryski, ill. by Tom Sankey. Text © 1983 by Camilla Gryski, ill. © 1983 by Tom Sankey. Reprinted by permission of William Morrow + Co.

Materials and Resources:

Ball, W.W.R. *Fun With String Figures.* New York: Dover, 1971.

Gryski, C. *Cat's Cradle, Owl's Eyes: A Book of String Games.* New York: Morrow, 1983.

Gryski, C. *Many Stars & More String Games.* New York: Morrow, 1985.

Gryski, C. *Super String Games.* New York: Morrow, 1987.

CHAPTER FOUR
CHANGE AND ADAPTATION

What can I say to my Omaha people? That is my main question. For two nights I have stayed awake looking for honest thoughts and true words to say. I knew my Omaha people would be afraid when they heard that the Bureau of Indian Affairs was thinking of making a great change in their lives. It is a poor life, but it is the only one they have to live. The only changes that will not frighten my Omaha people are the changes they make themselves...I think these respected officials are telling my people about how their life is to be changed, not asking whether they want it changed...If my Omaha people are allowed to make their own change, they will feel brave, proud, they will face the future standing up straight.

—Alfred W. Gilpin (Armstrong 1984)

CHANGE AND ADAPTATION

Change: v. to make or become different; to replace with another; n. the act, process or result of changing

Adaptation: n. made suitable or fit as for a new use or different conditions; adjustment or accommodation

Because the terms change and adaptation seem so closely allied, it seems important to differentiate clearly how they will be used in this model. According to the dictionary, the definitions above highlight the subtle, but important, difference.

In this chapter, the term change and adaptation are not used synonymously; *change* is stipulated to mean the act, process, or result of becoming different, whereas *adaptation* is considered to be the accommodation or the adjustment to change. Change, as defined above, can be as direct and abrupt as a governmental policy (Indian Removal Act of 1830) or an invention (guns) or exposure to a new culture (European) or phenomenon (horses). Change can also be a gradual process such as the extermination of the buffalo or the steady escalation of technological advances. Change requires or demands adaptation. *Change* will be used most frequently as a noun whereas adapt will be used as a verb or action and *adaptation* as the result of the action or response to change.

United States governmental policies forced or attempted to force indigenous peoples to adapt their cultures.

In a recent report on Indian education, ("Stuck on the Horizon?" 1989, 5) the following statement summarized the history of United States governmental policy as it related to Native Americans.

Since they first encountered white men in the 1500s, Native Americans have been subjected to policies that alternatively sought to exterminate and to "civilize" them—parting them, in the process, from their ancestral lands across the continent.

These policies and the resulting separation from the land meant that Indian people had to adapt their cultures—their ways of life.

Edward Spicer (1980) categorized the policies of the U.S. government toward American Indians into five distinct periods, each with a prevailing theme. These periods or themes are summarized as follows:

1. **Separation** (1625-1887) A period during which the prime objective was to remove Indians from the land that whites desired and draw boundaries between the two peoples. Example: Indian Removal Act—1830.

2. **Coercive assimilation** (1887-1934) Whites sought to replace Indian ways with their own ways and to help them become self-sufficient farmers and artisans, under condi-

tions dictated by whites. Example: Dawes General Allotment Act—1887.

3. **Tribal restoration, Phase I** (1934-1953) Whites made an about-face and encouraged Indians to maintain their corporate tribal existence if they chose to do so. Example: Indian Reorganization Act—1934

4. **Termination** (1952-1968) The objective was to break off all relationships of protection and assistance with the federal government. Example: see Gilpin quotation above.

5. **Tribal restoration, Phase II** (1968—present). Tribal corporate adaptation to American society was again encouraged and cultural choice was reaffirmed. Example: Indian Self-Determination Act—1975.

Each of these major policy themes, *separation, coercive assimilation, termination,* and even *tribal restoration,* demanded a response of a subjugated or conquered people to the wishes and demands of the conquerer. The survival of Native Americans is eloquent testimony on their ability to adapt—to the physical environment, to evolving technology, to another culture, and to political, economic, and historical realities. We must recognize that Native American people have demonstrated a remarkable ability to survive under oppressive and discriminatory governmental policies. It is also imperative to acknowledge that legislated or coercive change and subsequent adaptation have often resulted in turmoil, disruption, and social disorganization with devastating, long-term, and possibly irreversible effects.

> In our intercourse with the Indians it must always be borne in mind that we are the most powerful party...We...claim the right to control the soil which they occupy, and we assume that it is our duty to coerce them if necessary, into the adoption and practice of our habits and customs.
>
> —Columbus Delano (Spicer 1983, 235)

In Chapter Six, we will examine the current issues facing Native American people. We can view these issues as (1) confrontation of the problems that have resulted from inability or unwillingness to adapt to change, or inappropriate or dysfunctional adaptations, and (2) powerful leadership strategies to be developed and executed by Native Americans for future adaptations that are congruent with Indian tradition and values and rapid social change.

When the environment or technology change, cultures adapt.

This powerful principle is easier to teach than others simply because the everyday lives of young people reverberate with change—changes in family structure, changes in location and, changes in technology. We consider these changes "normal" in human lives today. Because these concrete and obvious changes in all students' experiences are easy to discuss, skillful teachers are able to use them to develop an understanding of social science generalizations.

In teaching about Native Americans we should stress this generalization in order to assist students in making connections between the ways in which the environment and technological development have influenced cultural development and the issues that are facing contemporary Native peoples. Again, the emphasis is upon helping students with understanding cause and effect relationships and the influences that affect all human ways of living.

History is replete with examples of how Native American peoples have adapted to changes in the environment and in technology. Let us consider a few.

ENVIRONMENT

Changes in the physical environment resulted in significant cultural adaptations when Native American people relocated either voluntarily or involuntarily. Involuntary or forced relocation has been common throughout Indian history. Some of the well-known forced relocations are The Long Walk of the Navajo (1864) and The Trail of Tears of the Five Civilized Tribes (1838-1839), during the separation period.

Since the 1700s changes in the social environment resulted in cultural adaptations and can be demonstrated by major political reorganizations of groups of Indian people. The past and present influences of religion can also be viewed as cultural reorganizations or adaptations. First, we will take a brief look at two major phenomena, the League of the Iroquois as political reorganization in response to European influence, and the Handsome Lake religion as a religious reorganization.

THE LEAGUE OF THE IROQUOIS

One of the major adaptive strategies of the Indian people was political confederation. Some confederations were successful as a means of survival and some were not. The League of the Iroquois (the five nations of the Mohawk, Oneida, Seneca, Cayuga, and Onondaga) was unique and very powerful for a period of time. The confederation of these five nations, and ultimately a sixth nation, the Tuscarora, rose to its greatest power between 1644-1700.

The program of the Iroquois had two parts: (1) to subordinate all surrounding Indian nations, and (2) to resist any domination by the French. Because of the cooperative efforts of the confederation, it was able to maintain a unified action against both groups. This type of organization was not to be found among any other Indian groups at that time. Ultimately, as the Americans demonstrated their military power, the league disintegrated, and there was no longer unanimity among the Iroquois.

The organizational structure of the Iroquois has had substantial influence on the development of democratic principles embodied in our Constitution. The influence of this confederacy is still manifested in our way of life.

THE HANDSOME LAKE RELIGION

About 1800, an elderly Seneca Indian, Ganeodiyo or Handsome Lake, began to be aware of new teachings that were being revealed to him in unusual dreams. In these dreams, supernatural beings revealed to him a new way of life for the Seneca. Handsome Lake began to share these teachings with others and the religion spread quickly. His teachings became known to the Iroquois as Kaiwiyoh, referred to in English as the Code of Handsome Lake.

In the history of the Indians of the Northeast Region, this was the time of lack of purpose and social organization. What Handsome Lake presented was not so much a new religion but a way to renew the traditions of the Iroquois and to bring about their moral regeneration. His teachings were a synthesis of many of the new ways of the Anglo and the old ways of the Iroquois. In many ways they accommodated Anglo-European ways while affirming Iroquois beliefs and values. The Code of Handsome Lake made it possible to remain Iroquois in identity and in religious beliefs, and still adapt to new occupations, family lifeways, and interpersonal relationships. The following quotation is an excerpt from the Code of Handsome Lake (Spicer 1983, 257):

> The white man keeps horses and cattle. Now there is no evil in this for they are a help to his family. So if he dies his family has the stock for help. Now all this is right if there is no pride. No evil will follow this practice if the animals are well fed, treated kindly and not over worked. Tell this to your people.

Handsome Lake was considered a great innovator and his teachings were quite revolutionary. The Code of Handsome Lake is still recited today in the Northeast Region and is a living religion that continues to guide Native American people in adapting to the dominant culture while maintaining an Indian worldview.

TECHNOLOGY

Each of us is sensitive to the influences of technology on our lives. Recently, we have become familiar with the effects of such things as acid rain, resource scarcity and depletion, the demise of family farms, personal computers, VCR and fax machines, laser beams, heart transplants, and liposuction! Most of those words and ideas were not known or seemed inconceivable ten years ago. As we have moved from an agricultural to an industrial society, and then to an information society, we have changed how we live in fundamental ways. As a result of technology, our problems have changed as well. Similarly, as Europeans introduced certain technologies to Native peoples and as the larger society has developed and adapted to newer technologies, Native American cultures have been similarly affected.

Two examples illustrate this adaptation—the effects of the introduction of horses and the emerging occupations and economic bases of some Indian tribes and people.

HORSES

The horse changed dramatically the lives of the people of the Plains. Before the horse, families moved their possessions with the help of dogs. Dogs bore packs or dragged frames of sticks (travois) loaded with baggage. Possessions, therefore, were light and limited.

After the introduction of the horse, the travois could be as long as 30 feet and could carry large hide-covered tipis. Food, such as dried meat and pemmican, could be accumulated and moved in large quantities. Not only was the hunt easier on horseback, but the horse also enabled people to travel large distances to find game; consequently food was more abundant. Life became easier, more settled than before, with new tools, new clothes, and spare time.

Horses created an additional purpose for war. Ownership of horses determined a warrior's fortune and consequently capturing horses became the goal of war. War societies with elaborate rituals and ceremonies became common. With horse prosperity, tribes could gather on occasion for special observances and ceremonies, bringing an additional social aspect to their lives.

Finally, the horse brought time to think and to dream. The combination of infinite space on the prairie and the horse seemed to encourage religion and the development of metaphysical beliefs. Religion was and remains a significant part of the Plains Indians' lives. Similarly, the horse revolutionized other Native American cultures and was an adaptation that was perceived as improving the quality of life.

OCCUPATIONS

Some of the most successful economic endeavors of Indian people, particularly those living on reservations are far from traditional. The Iroquois have become renowned for their skill and courage in dangerous structural steel construction on New York City skyscrapers. The Navajo are developing the rich natural resources of oil, coal, gas, and uranium that lie deep under their mesas. The Apache have developed forestry industries and built ski resorts. Other tribal people have developed some economic self-sufficiency in encouraging tourism, developing cooperatives for the production and sale of Indian arts and crafts, and sponsoring bingo games on reservation land. These occupations acknowledge that Native Americans are not only part of our historic past, but are vital participants in our political and economic present and future.

It is not realistic to expect Native Americans to remain the same. Continuous change has been a universal condition in human society throughout all time.

The tribal systems are static in that all movement is related to all other movement—that is, harmonious and balanced or unified; they are not static in the sense that they do not allow or accept change. Even a cursory examination of tribal systems will show that all have undergone massive changes while retaining those characteristics of outlook and experience that are the bedrock of tribal life. (Allen 1986, 56)

Perhaps this quotation is sufficient to remind teachers that tribal traditions, experiences, and fundamental values form the enduring structure of Native American culture. Nonetheless, these cultures, like all others, have adapted and will continue to adapt to changing social and physical environmental and technological changes. To teach only that Native Americans constituted harmonious and balanced cultures of the past without teaching that they are dynamic and evolutionary cultures of the present, perpetuates another kind of subtle racism (Kopper 1986, 281).

> Who but an out-of-touch intellectual would arrogantly assert that the American Indian, alone among peoples, should not change but should remain a textbook example of "the ethnographic present?" The Indian's survival in the contemporary world, different as that world is from the form uncovered by prehistoric archaeology and post-settlement ethnography, is itself a vindication of their Indianness. (Kopper 1986, 281)

References

Allen, P.G. *The Sacred Hoop*. Boston, Mass.: Beacon Press, 1986.

Armstrong, V.I., ed. *I Have Spoken: American History Through the Voices of the Indians*. Athens, Ohio: Swallow Press, 1984.

Garaway, M.K. *The Old Hogan*. Cortez, Colo.: Mesa Verde Press, 1986.

Johansen, B. *Forgotten Founders*. Ipswich, Mass.: Gambit Publishers, 1982.

Kickingbird, K. *Indians and the U.S. Constitution: A Forgotten Legacy*. Washington, D.C.: Institute for the Development of Indian Law, 1987.

Kopper, P. *The Smithsonian Book of North American Indians Before the Coming of the Europeans*. New York: Smithsonian Books, 1986.

McAllester, D., and S. McAllester. *Hogans: Navajo Houses and House Songs*. Middletown, Conn.: Wesleyan University Press, 1980.

Osinski, A. *The Navajo*. Chicago, Ill.: Children's Press, 1987.

Schaaf, G. *The Great Law of Peace and the Constitution of the United States of America*. North Bend, Wash.: Gregory Schaaf, n.d.

Spencer, P. U. "The Great Tree of Peace—Symbol of the Iroquois Confederacy—Part of Our National Heritage." *Kui Tatk*. Washington, D.C.: Native American Science Education Association, Fall 1987.

Spicer, E. H. *A Short History of the Indians of the United States*. Malabar, Fl.: Robert E. Krieger, 1983.

Spicer, E. H. *The American Indians*. Cambridge, Mass.: Belknap Press of Harvard University Press, 1980.

"Stuck in the Horizon?" *Education Week*, August 2, 1989.

Lesson Plans

Grade Level: Secondary

Basic Concepts: Change and adaptation

Organizing Generalization: The Great Law of Peace of the Iroquois Confederacy developed out of a need to terminate hostilities among themselves and develop a cooperative political structure.

Culture Area: Northeast

Time Period: Pre-European Contact

Background: After years of intertribal hostility, the Five Tribes, (Mohawk, Seneca, Cayuga, Oneida, and Onondaga) of the Northeast came together to form a confederacy which was governed by the Great Law of Peace. The men usually credited with developing democracy in the United States drew heavily upon this wisdom and experience in developing the Albany Plan, the Articles of Confederation, and eventually, the Constitution. These Americans had new realities to which they had to adapt, as did the Native Americans in an earlier time.

Objectives:

Knowledge (Content)

Students will:

1. give examples of how democracy was developed in the Great Law of Peace;

2. give examples of how democracy was developed in the United States Constitution; and

3. describe the historical context of each of these documents, acknowledging the need for change in political structures in each period of history.

Skills

Students will:

1. chart the similarities in the Great Law of Peace and the Constitution; and

2. examine cause and effect relationships in terms of social and political change and adaptation.

Values (Organic)

Students will:

1. appreciate that problems take study, creativity, hard work, compromise, and changes in attitude before solutions are found;

2. be cognizant of historical bias when they understand that democracy in America was an outgrowth of Native American wisdom as well as developed from the thinking of European philosphers of the Enlightenment;

3. learn that change is a constant and when adaptation is accomplished with deliberation and foresight, it can have an enduring effect; and

4. realize the value of primary sources in social science research.

Activities:

1. If possible, obtain a classroom set of *The Great Law of Peace and the Constitution of the United States of America* (Schaaf n.d.). This is a small pamphlet, but it requires considerable thought and study.

2. The teacher should lead a discussion on the social and political environments at the time of the development of both agreements, with students expected to take notes. An outline should be provided for them on an overhead projector.

3. Students will form study groups to list, as succinctly as possible and in their own words, examples of democratic principles in both the Great Law of Peace and the Constitution. The pamphlet, described above, can be used as a guide along with other resources. Written summaries should be submitted by each student.

EXTENSIONS

1. Students can compare the United Nations Charter and the Great Law of Peace to determine if the wisdom that brought peace to the tribes could be applied to current world problems.

2. Analyze current proposals that have been discussed as Constitutional Amendments (Equal Rights Amendment, abortion, flag desecration) and examine social, political, and economic changes that have prompted these proposals. Should the Constitution be adapted? Are there solutions other than Constitutional amendments? What would be the long-term effects of these proposed amendments?

3. After reading Paula Underwood Spencer's *Great Tree of Peace* (1987), students could write a similar poem about the Constitution. This poem could also be presented as a choral reading.

4. Individuals may be interested in pursuing the study of the importance of symbolism and wampum to the Iroquois Confederacy.

Evaluation:

Students will rewrite the appropriate section in their textbook or other classroom resources to include appropriate credit to the Great Law of Peace.

Materials and Resources:

Johansen, B. *Forgotten Founders*. Ipswich, Mass.: Gambit Publishers, 1982.

Kickingbird, K. *Indians and the U.S. Constitution: A Forgotten Legacy* Washington, D.C.: Institute for the Development of Indian Law, 1987. Brochure, booklet and video available from 1104 Glyndon Street S.E., Vienna, VA 22180.

Schaaf, G. *The Great Law of Peace and The Constitution of the United States of America*. North Bend, Wash.: Gregory Schaaf, n.d. Order from Dr. Gregory Schaaf, 44626 S.E. 151 Place, North Bend, WA 98045.

Spencer, P. U. "The Great Tree of Peace—Symbol of the Iroquois Confederacy—Part of Our National Heritage."

Kui Tatk, Fall 1987. Order from Native American Science Education Association, 1333 H Street N.W., Washington, DC 20005.

The Great Law of Peace and the Constitution of the United States of America. *Aksesasne Notes*. Rooseveltown, N.Y.: Mohawk Nation.

THE GREAT TREE OF PEACE

The Confederacy of Five (Iroquois) Nations began with the Covenant—

The Covenant was the basis for the Law.
The Law was Peace.
Peace was a Way of Life.
   characterized by Wisdom and Graciousness.
Wisdom sees Past, Present and Future at a glance.
Graciousness takes every individual understanding
into consideration as one part of the whole.
Understanding which is necessary for Peace.

These concepts are symbolized
   by The Great Tree of Peace.
This Tree signifies the Law.
The Law is Peace among all Nations
   which subscribe to the Constitution.
This Law undergirds the Constitution.

The branches of this Great Tree signify shelter,
   giving each Individual
      protection and security under the Law.
These branches are tended
   by Those among the People who are Men.

The roots of this Great Tree
   stretch to the Four Corners of the Earth—
   signify the possible extension of this law and this Peace
   to any of Earth's children willing to accept them.

These White Roots of Peace are tended
   by Those among the People who are Women.
Eagle—perched aloft—
   sees Past, Present, and Future at a glance,
   signifies watchfulness, wisdom, eternal vigilance.

Daganaweda uprooted The Tree,
   buried all weapons of war,
   replacing The Tree to grow
   and to shelter many Nations.
So be it.

Daganaweda speaks through the People—
   His hands are People's hands
   His voice is the People's voice,
   His wisdom is our wisdom.

—Turtle Woman Singing
(Paula Underwood Spencer)

Grade Level: Intermediate

Basic Concepts: Change and adaptation

Organizing Generalization: When technology changes, cultures change.

Culture Area: Southwest

Time Period: Contemporary

Background: This particular lesson can be useful in (1) dispelling the idea that Indians belong to the past, (2) presenting Native Americans in non-stereotypical roles and as people who are assuming leadership roles within their own culture (graduate student in anthropology), and (3) illustrating how it is possible to adapt to technological advances while maintaining traditional cultural values and ways of living. It is also important to realize that factors other than convenience often determine choices that we make. The lesson can easily be adapted and integrated with a science unit on solar energy. (See adaptation of "CU Hogans Combine Science, Navajo Life" at end of this lesson plan.)

Objectives:

Knowledge (Content)

Students will:

1. describe the relationship of the traditional hogan with the physical environment, the way the hogan is arranged for daily living, the spiritual beliefs and values associated with the hogan, and the ceremonial uses of the hogan;

2. become familiar with the climatic conditions of the reservation, the resources available to homes, (electricity, water and, wood) and the extended family structure of the Navajo. These factors partially determine how Navajo people have constructed their dwellings;

3. become familiar with the configuration of modern sheep camps on the Navajo reservation. This usually consists of a modern type of dwelling, a traditional hogan, and a shade house; and

4. list the advantages and disadvantages of each type of hogan and determine whether, in their opinion, the solar hogan is a positive adaptation to technological change.

Skills

Students will:

1. use a variety of information gathering strategies;

2. compare and contrast a traditional hogan with the solar hogan; and

3. use a decision-making strategy.

Values (Organic)

Students will:

1. learn about some of the important values of the Navajo people;

2. understand that it is possible to adapt to technological change and maintain cultural values; and

3. realize that values other than convenience or comfort can influence decisions.

Activities:

1. Read, or have students read, the attached newspaper article.

2. To initiate the lesson, ask students to think for a moment what life would be like if their homes did not have electricity or water. Then ask each student in order, round-robin fashion, to give an example of how living in a home without technology could be:

   a. positive

   b. interesting

   c. negative

3. To stimulate inquiry, ask students to discuss whether or not they think a solar hogan is a good idea. Would this technological adaptation be preferable to traditional or other modern dwellings? With guidance, students will discover that they do not have enough information to make a reasonable, rational, and culturally sensitive judgment. The teacher should lead students to raise such questions as:

   a. What is the traditional hogan like? How do families live there?

   b. How would life be different in a solar hogan?

   c. What is the climate of the Navajo Reservation? Is there adequate sunshine? How cold does it usually get? What resources are readily available for heating and cooking?

   d. What information do we need to know about this particular technological change? Is it costly to build and maintain?

   e. Why was it important to have a medicine man conduct a ceremony?

   f. What do we know about the spiritual beliefs of the Navajo regarding the hogan?

   g. How would the solar hogan change a way of life?

5. After students have had an opportunity for discussion, make a large chart with the following labels.

   What We Know

   What We Want

   How We Will Get To Learn Information

6. After research activities to answer the questions on the chart, ask students, in pairs, to answer why or why not, in their opinion the solar hogan is a positive adaptation to technological change.

EXTENSIONS

1. Discuss how technology affects our lives in positive and negative ways.

2. Many science experiments could be developed in this lesson. For example, how does solar energy work? Is it cost efficient? How does it affect the environment?

Evaluation:

Students should be able to make a reasoned judgment about the value of the solar hogan.

Materials and Resources:

Many books, filmstrips, and videos portray traditional Navajo life. Actual photographs of the different types of hogans would be useful.

Garaway, M.K. *The Old Hogan*. Cortez, Colo.: Mesa Verde Press, 1986.

McAllester, D., and S. McAllester. *Hogans: Navajo Houses and House Songs*. Middletown, Conn.: Wesleyan University Press, 1980.

CU HOGANS COMBINE SCIENCE, NAVAJO LIFE

Kevin McCullen—*Rocky Mountain News*, Boulder Bureau, October 7, 1989

BOULDER—A Navajo medicine man yesterday blessed three University of Colorado hogans with prayers and songs.

Gov. Roy Romer declared yesterday "Colorado Solar Hogan Project Day" in recognition of completion of a University of Colorado project praised by speakers as combining traditional Navajo housing with modern technology.

Later in the day, a Southern Ute medicine man blessed a renamed university dormitory, Cheyenne Arapaho Hall, in another ceremony.

George Bluehorse, a Navajo medicine man from New Mexico, blessed three hogans as University officials and Native American students, gathered inside each of the circular structures.

Many of the estimated 200 spectators listened to Bluehorse offer prayers and song to instill the Navajo spirit in the hogans. "This is usually only conducted for family members. But we were all one huge family today. George brought our Navajo spirit to the dedication," said Charlie Cambridge, a Navajo graduate student in anthropology and the driving force behind the hogan project.

The hogans represent a marriage of ancient culture and modern technology. "One sustains the other," said CU Chancellor Jim Corbridge.

In January, several Navajo students plan to move into the largest hogan, which contains photovoltaic cells to generate electricity and a small indoor garden. Sensors placed in the hogan walls will monitor energy use.

Cambridge, a Navajo, and architect Dennis Holloway of the CU College of Environmental Design, conceived the project several years ago. They nurtured it throughout the past year with help from state and CU officials and supplies and labor from students and community volunteers that Holloway dubbed, "Hogan's heroes."

Cambridge and Holloway hope to convince tribal housing officials to adopt the solar hogan method to build homes that combine cultural relevance with energy efficiency.

Grade Level: Primary

Basic Concepts: Change and adaptation

Organizing Generalization: Navajo people live differently now than they did in the past. They have been forced to change old ways; they have learned new things from other cultures; and they have developed some new and improved ways of meeting their needs.

Culture Area: Southwest

Time Period: Pre-European Contact, Post-European Contact

Background: One way to demonstrate how a culture has changed through time as a result of contact with other cultures, the inventiveness of the people, and the effects of technology is by studying their food. Food also has inherent interest for young children. The Navajo people have experienced several distinct periods:

Contemporary foods of the Navajo include the traditional foods, foods that were adapted from government rations (from the time at Fort Sumner to the present), foods that are now possible because of electricity and refrigeration in homes, new supermarkets located near settlements, and television and transportation bringing the common culture into Navajo homes. All of these influences pervade the Navajo diet and demonstrate, in concrete terms, how cultures change.

a traditional economy	gatherers	seeds, pinon nuts, berries, cacti, small animals, and game
an intermediate economy	agriculturalists animal husbandry government rations	foods above, corn and squash sheep and cattle white flour, and sugar
a contemporary economy	all of the above	foods above with the additional factors of poverty, and technological advances such as refrigeration, transportation, and television

Objectives:

Knowledge (Content)

Students will:

1. identify traditional Navajo foods and explain why this was so; and

2. identify contemporary Navajo foods and explain why this is so.

Skills

Students will:

work cooperatively to plan, prepare, and serve a Navajo meal.

Values (Organic)

Students will:

1. appreciate how important traditional food is to all cultures; and

2. understand that Navajo children are likely to eat the same foods as they do now. ("American" fast food restaurants now serve the reservation, and fry bread is likely to become the Navajo "Big Mac"!)

Activities:

1. Create a bulletin board that depicts reservation life—location, desert scenes, traditional and contemporary homes, sheep herding, school buses (school lunches), horses, trucks, trading posts, supermarkets and so on.

2. An excellent book for young children is *The Navajo* (Osinski 1987). This book is written in language that is easily understood and there are excellent photographs. The text emphasizes change, illustrating traditional and contemporary ways. This book should be read by the teacher. Excellent films, filmstrips, and videos are also available. Point out and discuss the three periods; traditional, intermediate, and contemporary.

3. If there is an Indian Center in the area, an Indian speaker, or exchange with Indian children should be arranged so that children can be with contemporary Indian children and visit with someone who can talk about old ways.

4. Class discussion and activities should focus on change—the bulletin board could be rearranged to classify old ways and new ways for Navajo people. Children should be encouraged to think of their own traditions and traditional food. Include foods of other cultures that they eat that are new to them.

5. A culminating activity will be a Navajo Taco lunch. On a chart or another bulletin board, students can identify which parts of the meal are from the traditional economy (turkey and beans), the intermediate economy (white flour, baking powder, dried milk, cheese), and the contemporary economy (lettuce, tomatoes).

EXTENSIONS

1. Make another bulletin board with pictures and recipes of traditional foods that children have brought from home.

2. Investigate the importance of sheep to the Navajo.

3. Children should be reading legends and stories of Southwestern Indians.

Evaluation:

Children should be able to distinguish between traditional food and contemporary food and explain why Navajo people still have traditional food and also now have new foods. This can be done with a classifying activity.

Materials and Resources:

Osinski, A. *The Navajo*. Chicago, Ill.: Children's Press, 1987.

NAVAJO TACO

(Navajo Chinle Agency, Arizona)

FRY BREAD

4 1/2 C. all-purpose flour

1 T. baking powder

2 T. non-fat dry milk powder

1 t. salt

1 1/2 C. warm water

1 C. vegetable oil for frying

1. Combine flour, baking powder, dry milk powder, and salt. Gradually add warm water and mix with dry ingredients to form a soft firm ball. Knead in bowl or on a lightly floured surface until smooth—about 10 minutes.

2. Separate dough into 8-10 small pieces and make circles of dough about 3/8 inches thick. Put a hole into the center.

3. Slip dough rounds into hot fat and fry, turning once, about 2 minutes on each side, until puffy and brown. Drain on paper towel.

4. Top warm fried bread with Chili Topping. Garnish each with shredded lettuce, tomatoes, and onions.

CHILI TOPPING

1 1/2 lb. browned ground turkey

1 – 2 T. chili powder

2 C. cooked beans

1 1/2 C. shredded American cheese

Combine ingredients

CHAPTER FIVE
CONFLICT AND DISCRIMINATION

Before our white brother came to civilize us we had no jails. Therefore, we had no criminals. You can't have criminals without a jail. We had no locks or keys, and so we had no thieves. If a man was so poor that he had no horse, tipi, or blanket, someone gave him these things. We were too uncivilized to set much value on personal belongings. We wanted to have things only in order to give them away. We had no money, and therefore a man's worth couldn't be measured by it. We had no written law, no attorneys or politicians, therefore we couldn't cheat. We were really in a bad way before the white man came, and I don't know how we managed to get along without the basic things which, we are told, are absolutely necessary to make a civilized society.

—Lame Deer of the Lakotas (Fire and Erdoes 1972)

CONFLICT AND DISCRIMINATION

Conflict: A clash between hostile or opposing elements or ideas.

Prejudice: An opinion for or against something without just grounds or sufficient knowledge.

Stereotype: A standardized mental picture held in common by members of a group and representing an over-simplified opinion, affective attitude, or uncritical judgment.

Discrimination: Difference in treatment or favor on a basis other than individual merit.

Conflict often occurs when two groups of people with different world views come together. People develop different values, beliefs about life, and sense of the meaning of things as they work out their survival. In the centuries before they met, Europeans and Native Americans had developed very different lifeways. The lack of reconciliation of those differences has produced 500 years of conflict. Because of the overwhelming numbers of Europeans, their advanced technology, and some of the values they held, Native Americans continually have been the losers in the battle for control of their own destiny.

This chapter will examine the values and attitudes that produced the European prejudice and the subsequent discrimination that has characterized their treatment of the Native American.

Differences in cultural values between Native Americans and Europeans and the dominant culture from the early contact to the present have caused prejudice, discrimination, and conflict.

When the Europeans began their search for riches in the Far East in the 15th century, they had already developed a value system that was far different from that of the indigenous peoples they were to encounter in the Americas. Some of these guiding values were:

- The spirit of capitalism they embraced meant competition, wealth, and the use of whatever natural resources they needed. Governments of many nations engaged in concerted efforts to seize sources of new wealth.

- The duality of right and wrong undergirded their beliefs. As possessors of the "truth," it was their duty to convert those who disagreed with them. There was a strong sense of the need to dominate "men of color" throughout the world.

- Their belief that the spirit of worldwide expansionism gave them the right to claim the lands of others. Although people came to North America for many reasons, one significant factor was the need for more land.

- The use of military force was common in Europe to gain both political as well as economic power. They used military power and advanced technology to conquer and destroy lands and people (Josephy 1986).

On the other hand, the Native American had developed a far different system of basic values.

- Life was not competitive; it was cooperative and the people in a community worked together for the survival and well-being of the entire group.

- Since the metaphysical manifested wisdom in different ways to each group, there was no single "truth" and no system of belief to which all needed to adhere.

- There was no shortage of resources because their ancestors had learned the proper ceremonies to ensure the necessities of survival from nature and had passed these ceremonies on to each generation.

- Because there was communal support, there was no concept of ownership of land, air, water, or the resources of the earth. The necessities of life were to be shared, not owned.

- All of nature was sacred and was treated with reverence.

- Military exploits were not to destroy, but to prove valor, to gain prominence and prestige, or to avenge a wrong (fig. 5.1).

It is easy to see why these two value systems would clash. Native Americans did not value private ownership so they were bewildered when the Europeans took away their lands. The Europeans, on the other hand, found the beliefs in communal ownership naive and easy to exploit; they did not resist doing so. They considered taking lands as legitimate in terms of competition. The difficulty was, Native Americans did not understand this concept of competition. Land was sacred to the Native American, and land was what the European wanted to own. Out of this irreconcilable difference grew the prejudice held by the Europeans and the discriminatory behavior that has endured for 500 years. In the land issue, military might prevailed and the Europeans ultimately succeeded in dispossessing the Native Americans, making them a subject people.

Prejudice and discrimination toward Native American people is evidenced in past and present national government policy.

These policies have been divided into the same five themes (Spicer 1980) as were presented in the previous chapter. However, in this chapter we will present the evidence of overt prejudice and discrimination in national government policy toward Native Americans throughout United States history. With each change in policy, an example will be provided to demonstrate the effects of that policy.

Figure 5.1
(Adapted from Stone and DeNevi 1971)

INDIAN WAY OF LIFE	EUROPEAN/ANGLO WAY OF LIFE
Present Oriented Live in the present, living for today, not tomorrow.	*Future Oriented* Rarely satisfied with the present. Constantly looking to the future.
Lack of Time Consciousness Many tribes have no word for time, because there is always lots of time; no need to be punctual or on time; concept of "Indian Time" which means that a meeting set for 8:00 P.M. may not start until 10:00 P.M.	*Time Consciousness* Governed by the clock and the calendar, living closely scheduled, certain amount of time devoted to each activity.
Giving Not concerned with saving; air and land was free, food could not be saved because it would spoil—no need to save. Respected person is one who gives. Value not placed on one who has large savings, but on giving. Person who tries to accumulate goods is often feared.	*Saving* Save today so can better enjoy tomorrow; hold back a part of wealth so can develop more things—"a penny saved is a penny earned." School is looked upon as a system of long-term saving because it will increase earning power in the future.
Respect for Age Respect increases with age and the tried and trusted leader is usually an older person. Youth is often a handicap with young Indian leaders frequently complaining that they are not given positions of leadership that they feel qualified to hold.	*Emphasis on Youth* The non-Indian society places great importance on youth; advertising, books, and newspapers all stress the value of youth. How to look young, how to act young. Little consideration given to age.
Cooperation Indians place a value on working together, sharing, and cooperating. Failure to reach selected objectives is felt to result from failure to cooperate.	*Competition* The non-Indian believes competition is essential if not universal. Progress results from competition, and lack of progress may be synonymous with lack of competition.
Harmony with Nature Indians believe in living in harmony with nature. They accept the world and do not try to change it. If it fails to rain, or the crops fail to grow, it is, they believe, because the necessary harmony has been destroyed. Whenever harmony is restored, nature will respond.	*Conquest over Nature* The non-Indian society attempts to control the physical world, to assert mastery over it. For example, dams, rain-making, atomic energy, etc.

SEPARATION (1625-1887)

The policies of separation can be summarized as:

• Lands taken away from Native Americans crippled their ability to be self-sufficient.

• Forced removal took Indians away from the lands that were sacred to them.

Long before the federal government began its official policy, the colonies instituted a pragmatic policy of separation. Separation began in 1625 when the first deed was "signed" by Samoset giving ownership of 12,000 acres (4,858 hectares) to the English colonists (Brown 1970). Over a period of approximately 150 years, this kind of removal continued as colonial settlers moved westward.

Nowhere was there any interest in cohabiting the lands, or allowing Native Americans to participate in or co-create a "colonial" life.

After the ratification of the United States Constitution, the federal government assumed control of Indian lands and treaties. The legal status of the tribes became a controversial issue for the United States government. Were tribes sovereign nations or were they a conquered and subject people? Treaties are made only between sovereign nations and then must be ratified by the United States Senate. When violence erupted over land ownership, did Congress need to make formal declarations of war? In these situations, if Indian tribes were sovereign nations, then Congress needed to act.

Conversely, if Native Americans were a conquered and subject people, their citizenship status needed to be clarified. (This issue was not settled until 1924, when Indians were designated to be citizens of the United States.) The legal status of Native Americans was never clear or consistent within the framework of the Constitution. It appears that the founding fathers did not consider Native Americans to be under the jurisdiction of the Constitution. The policy of separation would indicate that they were considered as autonomous people.

The only consistent pattern adopted by the federal government was its pragmatic response to demands made by settlers as they moved west. Governmental actions during this period hardly concealed the intent to make it convenient and legal to take Indian lands. Perhaps the most well-known of these legal actions was the Cherokee Removal Act of 1838-1839. This poignant journey of the Cherokee is known as the "Trail of Tears" and the legal aspects of this removal continued to plague the courts for over 150 years.

In the 1830s, after prospectors discovered gold on the lands held by the Cherokee in Georgia, they brought pressure on the federal government to make this valuable land available for settlement. The Supreme Court handed down a decision in favor of the Cherokee Nation, and Justice John Marshall established the concept of "dependent domestic nations." The case affirmed the rights of Indian Nations to negotiate with the federal government regarding lands and their status was acknowledged as that of treaty-making partners. This implied separate status such as accorded any foreign nation. However, President Andrew Jackson challenged the Supreme Court and he proceeded to carry out a forced removal of the Five Civilized Tribes, completely disregarding their legal rights and their wishes to remain in their homeland. During this forced removal, one-fourth of the people died.

Those who survived were taken to Oklahoma and reservations were established for them. The reservation policy continued, as an extension of separation, until all the Native people had been subdued and were no longer a threat to the European settlers.

Until 1868, the government made treaties forcing land relinquishment. However, the legitimate authorities within the Indian tribes had not necessarily agreed to the treaties. Nor did the government honor the treaties when settlers demanding land applied pressure to abrogate them.

Until 1870, a branch of legal opinion sustained the legal rights of Indian peoples to make treaties. It originated with *Cherokee Nation v. Georgia* in 1831. It was paralleled by the more pragmatic policy to disregard these treaties. In 1871, Congress abandoned the treaty-making policy and, aware of the inevitable destruction of the tribes of the Plains Region, assumed an open policy of unbridled power establishing reservations for the displaced tribes. This action separated the Native Americans from the settlers.

When Native Americans became wards of the government on reservations, they lost all rights of self-determination. With a system of alien laws to control their lives, self-government was destroyed and the Bureau of Indian Affairs (B.I.A.) assumed responsibility for all aspects of Indian life. Of note is the origin of the B.I.A. as a branch of the War Department.

In the period during and following the Civil War (1861-1890), the military determined settlement activity in the Plains Region and in the Southwest Region, placing Native Americans in a subordinate position. As demand for Pacific coast trails to secure land and gold increased, the military forced Native Americans to withdraw from their traditional homelands. By the 1860s the Europeans coveted even the lands of the Plains, and eventually the deserts of the Great Basin and Southwest. The government then forced reservation life on the nomadic tribes. The removal of the Navajo to the Bosque Redondo in eastern New Mexico was one of the those forced removals.

From 1860-1868, the United States Army, in the territory newly-acquired from Mexico (the result of the treaty of Guadalupe Hildago that ended the Mexican War in 1848), attempted to round up the Navajo people and settle them on a reservation at Bosque Redondo. General Kit Carson, a former friend of the Navajo, was hired to capture them and bring them into the reservation. The Navajos were promised that supplies awaited them at the fort. Carson resorted to a "scorched earth policy" in the farmlands of the Navajo to starve them into submission. Mortality statistics are similar to the Cherokee Trail of Tears. As each group of Navajo was forced to surrender, they trudged the 300 miles of the Long Walk to the reservation.

Bosque Redondo (ironically, the name means Round Forest) was uninhabitable. The first Navajos to be relocated began to slip away because they could not find clean drinking water, nor could they grow crops. Armed guards were posted to shoot on sight any Indian attempting to escape. In September 1866, the last of the Navajo chiefs, Manuelito, arrived with a small band of followers. The Navajo were more fortunate than others, for within a few weeks, a new superintendent was assigned to the reservation. He found "The water (to be) black and brackish, scarcely bearable to the taste, and said by the Indians to be unhealthy, because one-fourth of their population have been swept off by disease" (Brown 1970).

It took two years for the government to study the problems at Bosque Redondo before the Navajo could return to their lands. They were one of the few fortunate tribes *allowed* to have a reservation on lands they had previously inhabited.

COERCIVE ASSIMILATION (1887-1934)

Once tribal people had been placed on reservations (not unlike prisoners of war), settlers began to demand reservation lands. In the Allotment Act or Dawes Act of 1887, all Indian individuals were forced to take 160 acres of reservation land. The purpose of this legislation was to make them into responsible farmers. After this allotment, any surplus of reservation lands could then be sold by the federal government to new settlers. The urgency to enforce this law came from the pressure of these immigrants who were eager to acquire land under the Homestead Act of 1862.

Allotment and other assimilation policies were intended to "force Indians into the cultural mold of what was then the dominant set of values in the United States" (Spicer 1983). Governmental policies intended to make Indian people relinquish their traditional values and ways of living and accept the ways of the independent Anglo-American farmer. The B.I.A. school system and missionary schools were established to teach Indian children the English language and to learn how to live like Anglo-Americans. Children were forced to attend boarding schools year-round so that their families could have little influence and they would more easily forget their own traditions. Severely punished if they spoke their own language, their hair was cut and they were taught to eat, dress, and behave like whites. They were also converted to various Christian religions.

The Five Civilized Tribes were exempt from the Allotment Act because they held a treaty that stated that they could not be forced again to relinquish land they held. They succeeded in maintaining their independence in Oklahoma until 1898. Ultimately the government ignored the treaty and Congress passed the Curtis Act, which not only forced allotment but also terminated self-government for these tribes. Their school system, which had produced more college graduates than the state of Texas, was destroyed and replaced by a far inferior system administered by the B.I.A. (Deloria 1974). Armed posses were sent to capture Indian people to force them to sign allotment papers. As late as 1910, only 10 percent of the Cherokee had signed. Unfortunately, this did not deter the government from taking their lands.

According to some students of Indian affairs, this is the most destructive period of Indian history. As the culture was systematically attacked and poverty became more pervasive, Native Americans began to lose hope, self-reliance, and energy, and the identity they had maintained during the 19th century struggles diminished.

Even with the concerted governmental effort and the resultant human suffering, the policies of coercive assimilation did not achieve their goals because significant cultural and political differences remained between the Native Americans and the settlers with European backgrounds. In 1928, the Brookings Institution published the findings of a major study, the Meriam Survey, in *The Problem of Indian Administration*. The report detailed the failure of the B.I.A., the missionary efforts, and the increasing poverty and disease found among Native Americans. In 1934, the government initiated a new policy.

TRIBAL RESTORATION—PHASE I (1934-1953)

The publicity of the Meriam Survey prompted Congress to pass the Reorganization Act (Wheeler-Howard Act 1934). Like other major pieces of legislation, the final act did not resemble the original document proposed by John Collier, one of the most energetic political figures who worked on behalf of Native Americans in the 20th century. His all-encompassing bill was intended to restore Indian self-government and also provide for the restoration of languages, customs, and religious freedom. All of these basic human rights had been denied to tribal members during the harsh Allotment period. Many members of Congress did not want such far-reaching legislation, so when the bill became law, they amended it significantly. However, the legislation did provide for self-determination for the tribes and a reduction in the authority of the superintendencies of the B.I.A.

How then did Native Americans still suffer discrimination when it appeared as though the worst of the Allotment period had passed and that new legislation ensured fair treatment? We will take our example for this period from the field of education.

Until the Reorganization Act of 1934, the education of Indian children was the responsibility of the Bureau of Indian Affairs. With the advent of the Progressive Education movement, initiated by the philosophy of John Dewey, Collier had a framework within which to work. He maintained that Native American culture should be revitalized, and a new phase began in Indian education.

He devised a system to eliminate the boarding schools and to establish a system of day schools with students remaining in their own communities. When children had access to public schools, they were to be mainstreamed into the existing student body, with teachers paying special attention to their cultural differences and tribal customs.

Perhaps the idealism of this program doomed it before it began. The new policy demanded that teachers and administrators adjust and change basic attitudes in order to accommodate this new vision for Indian children. Long-held personal and professional attitudes and values are difficult to change. The program designed to retrain teachers proved inadequate. In addition, financial confusion over federal monies allotted to states made disbursement not only difficult but caused charges of unfairness and fraud.

Though the federal government took a decidedly different stand toward Native American problems during this period by instituting positive programs, and changed federal policy to be congruent with self-determination principles, it could not obliterate personal discrimination and prejudice. The important Johnson-O'Malley Bill, passed in 1934, gave the states the primary responsibility for educating Native American children. It seemed this would make the needs of the children more immediate and cultural differences could be better accommodated than in the past. However, the children did not receive what was mandated and intended by the new law.

Laws cannot force people to treat others with respect, leading Margaret Connell Szasz (1984, 105) to make the following statement:

The primary weakness in the Johnson-O'Malley program that prevented the Education Division from implementing its ideas can be summarized as follows: the poor quality of teachers and administrators; the hostile attitudes of communities; the public schools' greater interest in funding than in Indian students themselves; the diversity of conditions among and within the states; and the difficult relationships between state and federal administrators. All of these led to a type of education ill suited to the needs of the Indian child.

These issues are still confronting the parents and educators of Indian youth today.

TERMINATION (1952-1968)

"When a policy is used as a weapon to force cultural confrontation, then the underlying weakness of society is apparent. No society which has real and lasting values need rely on force for their propagation" (Deloria 1988). The policy of termination was not only an attempt by the government to force conformity and acculturation but also to reject responsibility for the tribes. In 1947, William Zimmerman, Acting Commissioner of Indian Affairs, proposed to terminate the federal government's responsibility to specific tribes. Originally, the purpose of his proposal was to save money for the government. The following four criteria were established to determine if a tribe was ready for termination:

1. a satisfactory degree of acculturation to white ways,
2. economic self-sufficiency of the tribe,
3. willingness of the tribe to dispense with federal aid, and
4. willingness of the state where the tribe resided to assume responsibility (Deloria 1988).

In 1952, Congress began to put the policy into effect. However, the four criteria used to determine which tribes should be terminated were not used in any of the cases.

The Menominee of Wisconsin had received a judgment against the government in a court battle prior to termination proceedings. The law authorized the disbursement of the funds which were then held as ransom until the tribe voted for termination. The voting procedures were irregular; there was no regulation on voter eligibility or an agreement on the percentage of the votes of registered tribal members needed to approve the policy. Since the early days of the Allotment, many tribal people had not voted in order to register their disapproval of a governmental policy. This practice was common in the democratic tribal proceedings. Consequently, only a fraction of the Menominee, those who were interested in the release of the money owed them by the government, voted in the crucial election. There is little evidence that these voters understood the ramifications of the Termination Plan.

If the government hoped to save federal money by termination, it was disappointed. Termination of the Menominee cost six million dollars for the federal government and one million dollars for the state of Wisconsin. A failing economy on the reservation, increases in infant mortality because of inadequate medical care and rampant tuberculosis made the "reservation become county" an economic and human disaster.

The policy was short-lived because the legislation was confusing and it was poorly implemented. In many cases, hearings were conducted without tribal representation and in most cases, extortion was used to obtain favorable votes. When Congress detained money awarded to tribes by judicial proceeding in order to force termination, tribal members ultimately surrendered and voted for termination in order to have the money released.

It becomes clear why none of Zimmerman's four criteria was ever used to designate the tribes that were suitable for termination. The tribes that Congress was so eager to terminate were not ready for termination, according to these established criteria.

TRIBAL RESTORATION—PHASE II (1968-PRESENT)

This phase initiated an ongoing effort to restore self-determination to Native Americans. As present policy, it will be discussed in Chapter 6.

> Like the miner's canary, the Indian marks the shift from fresh air to poison air in our political atmosphere...our treatment of Indians, even more than our treatment of other minorities, reflects the rise and fall of our treatment of other minorities, reflects the rise and fall of our democratic faith.
>
> —Felix Cohen, (*Indian Tribes: A Continuing Quest for Survival,* 1981)

Relations between Native Americans and the dominant culture have been characterized by exploiting Native Americans.

If national policy has been characterized by prejudice, discrimination, and exploitation, we must acknowledge that those actions were supported by the convenience of stereotyping. In this regard, Josephy (1986, 31) remarks:

Through the centuries, most Whites have cast all Indians in group images that have changed from time to time to suit new needs and conditions but have always been unreal. They have been regarded successively as innocent children of nature, noble savages, subhuman demons, untrustworthy thieves and murderers, stoic warriors, inferior and vanishing vestiges of the Stone Age, depraved drunkards, shiftless, lazy, humorless incompetents unable to handle their own affairs—almost anything but true-to-life, three-dimensional men, women, and children, as individualistic and human as any other people on earth.

These convenient stereotypes—none with positive connotation, usually enable others to justify discrimination and exploitation. Of particular alarm is the *still-reported* unjust treatment of Native Americans, particularly where Native Americans and Anglo-Europeans live near one another and when Anglo-Europeans covet their lands and resources. For example, in 1979, a deputy prosecutor stated, "When the Indians talk about rights, they should remember it's like a master-servant relationship. The Lord giveth and the Lord taketh away. This is the white man's case; there are more of us than there are of them" (Josephy 1986). When Indian people are seen as less than human, this kind of statement is more tolerable, when, indeed, it is intolerable.

Taken one step further, it is possible to justify taking Indian children from reservation homes to be adopted by non-Indian people, to publicly display sacred objects, to ridicule Indian languages and cultural ceremonies, and to exploit natural resources.

In fairness, stereotyping has another effect. It is interesting how, in the effort to right past wrongs, we have also romanticized Native Americans, also making them less than human. We often discuss the Native American as the first ecologists. Vine Deloria, Jr., has pointed out how Indians tend to despoil their reservations with casually tossed beer cans, auto carcasses left to deteriorate, and so on. There is evidence to indicate that, even in the past, Indians were not the careful steward of Mother Earth they are sometimes thought to be (Kopper 1986).

The fundamental issue of stereotyping is educational and one that teachers can confront by direct teaching and by carefully selecting educational materials. The current status of prejudice, discrimination, and stereotyping will be addressed in Chapters 6 and 7. However, it is fair to say that Native Americans still struggle to end the discrimination to which they have been subject and the prejudicial attitudes that sustain it.

I have heard talk and talk, but nothing is done.

Good words do not last long unless they amount to something.

Words do not pay for my dead people.

They do not pay for my country, now overrun by white men...

Good words will not give my people good health and stop them from dying.

Good words will not get my people a home where they can live in peace and take care of themselves.

I am tired of talk that comes to nothing.

It makes my heart sick when I remember all the good words

and broken promises...

—Chief Joseph (Armstrong 1984, 116)

References

Armstrong, V. I., ed. *I Have Spoken: American History Through the Voices of the Indians.* Athens, Ohio: Swallow Press, 1984.

Bernstein, B., and L. Blair, *Native American Crafts Workshop.* Belmont, Calif.: Pitman Learning, 1982.

Billard, J.B., ed. *The World of the American Indian.* Washington, D.C.: National Geographic Society, 1989.

Brown, D. *Bury My Heart at Wounded Knee.* New York: Pocket Books, 1970.

Cohen, F. S. "Erosion of Indian Rights 1950-1953: A Case Study in Bureaucracy." *Yale Law Journal* 62 (1953): 390.

Deloria, V., Jr. *Behind the Trail of Broken Treaties.* New York: Dell, 1974.

Deloria, V., Jr. *Custer Died for Your Sins: An Indian Manifesto.* Norman: University of Oklahoma Press, 1988.

Ever, L., ed. *Between Sacred Mountains: Navajo Stories and Legends from the Land.* Tucson: Sun Tracks and the University of Arizona Press, 1986.

Josephy, A.M., Jr. *Now That the Buffalo's Gone.* Norman: University of Oklahoma Press, 1986.

Kopper, P. *The Smithsonian Book of North American Indians Before the Coming of the Europeans.* New York: Smithsonian Books, 1986.

Meriam, L., et al. *The Problem of Indian Administration.* Baltimore, Md.: The Brookings Institution, 1928.

Moquin, W., and C. Van Doren, eds. *Great Documents in American Indian History.* New York: Praeger, 1973.

O'Dell, S. *Sing Down the Moon.* New York: Dell, 1970.

Prucha, F., ed. *Documents of United States Indian Policy.* Lincoln: University of Nebraska Press, 1975.

Spicer, E. H. *The American Indians.* Cambridge, Mass.: Belknap Press of Harvard University Press, 1980.

Spicer, E. H. *A Short History of the Indians of the United States.* Malabar, Fla.: Robert E. Krieger, 1983.

Stone, J.C., and D. P. DeNevi, eds. *Teaching Multi-Cultural Populations.* New York: D. Van Nostrand, 1971.

Szasz, M.C. *Education and the American Indian: The Road to Self-Determination.* Albuquerque: University of New Mexico Press, 1984.

Lesson Plans

Grade Level: Intermediate

Basic Concepts: Conflict, discrimination, and subjugation

Organizing Generalization: In the past, the Navajo people were treated as an inferior and subjugated people by the Anglo-European inhabitants of the southwest and by the United States Government. The government tried to relocate Navajo people from their land and to change their traditional ways of life—they wanted them to become Christian farmers. Cultural differences were in conflict and the changes were intolerable to the Navajo people.

Culture Area: Southwest

Time Period: Post-European Contact to 1890

Background: This lesson plan is based on the book *Sing Down the Moon* (O'Dell 1970). It is important to point out that there may be some historical inaccuracies, as the Spanish had left the Southwest before the Long Walk period. Specific fictional incidents in the book probably refer to the active slave trade practiced by the New Mexicans and some Indian tribes. However, the book does give an engaging personal perspective on the treatment of Native Americans by the Anglo-American citizens and settlers and the United States government. Because of its literary value, this book is particularly well suited to classrooms where a whole language or thematic approach to curriculum is used. The following lesson plan is based upon Chapters 19-22, which describe life at Fort Sumner at Bosque Redondo, after the Long Walk.

Objectives:

Knowledge (Content)

Students will:

1. describe daily life at Fort Sumner including (a) shelter, (b) food, (c) responsibilities of the women and men, and (d) ways they were required to adapt in order to survive; and

2. describe and give examples of how the Long Knives (U.S. Government soldiers) treated the Navajo people.

Skills

Students will:

contrast the traditional way of life of Bright Morning and the life imposed upon her at Fort Sumner.

Values (Organic)

Students will:

1. experience, through Bright Morning, the humiliation and inhumanity, endured by the Navajo during the Long Walk; and

2. understand the importance of each person's culture and how difficult it is to adopt the culture of another.

Activities:

1. The book consists of 23 short chapters that teachers can read to the students, or that students can read. This plan is based upon chapters 19-22.

2. Create a mural of Canyon de Chelly that illustrates the physical environment and the traditional ways of the Navajo.

3. Make a large map that shows the location of Canyon de Chelly and Fort Sumner at Bosque Redondo.

4. Ask students to form groups of 4-5 members. Each team will complete the following chart:

	Traditional	Fort Sumner
Shelter		
Food		
Clothing		
Roles of women		
Roles of men		

5. One member of each group will compile the group charts into a large classroom chart.

6. Using the chart as a guide, engage students in the following discussion.

   a. Why did Bright Morning want to return to the canyon? How did she prepare for the journey? How did they manage to survive the trip?

   b. What clues do you have on why the Navajo men were not willing to escape or fight the government troops?

   c. Why do you think Tall Boy did not want to escape? Why didn't he want to think of the canyon or the sheep?

   d. Why do you think the government wanted to change the way of life of the Navajo people?

   e. Do you think it was right to force the Navajo from their homeland?

7. The Long Walk is still bitterly remembered by the Navajo people. Ask the students to talk about the current meaning of these words:

   My father always told us that from the time of the Long Walk our ancestors' strongest advice was never to leave this land again, trade it, or sell it, because they suffered grief, tears, and death for their land (Evers 1986, 245).

EXTENSIONS

1. The Sand Creek Massacre is mentioned in this chapter. Some students may want to read more about this historical event.

2. Ghosts and witches are referred to as the causes of illness and death. Advanced readers will enjoy reading the

mystery novels by Tony Hillerman. He explains these Navajo beliefs in engaging ways throughout his books.

3. Read a biography of General Kit Carson. Questions to be asked might include:

   a. In your opinion, was General Carson a friend of the Navajo?

   b. Was General Carson admired by the people? If so why?

   c. Make a list of places that have been named for General Carson. (Carson City, Nevada, Carson National Park, etc.)

4. As a class, decide what Bright Morning might have named her son.

Evaluation:

1. Students will give five examples of how the government tried to change the Navajo at Fort Sumner and five examples of how the government treated them like a conquered people.

2. Because students are likely to identify and sympathize with Bright Morning, it is also likely that they would express strong feelings about her treatment. Teachers will want to extend this discussion to any inhumane treatment of one group of people toward another group, the bravery of Bright Morning, and toward the understanding of the right of all people to their cultural ways.

Materials and Resources:

- Map of the area from Canyon de Chelly to Bosque Redondo.

- Pictures of Canyon de Chelly. The Visitors Center, operated by the National Park Service and located at Canyon de Chelly in Chinle, Arizona, has many books, materials, and maps about the canyon.

O'Dell, S. *Sing Down the Moon.* New York: Dell, 1970.

An Ancient Gift (1982). A 15 minute video produced by the national Endowment for the Humanities, Northern Arizona Museum, Flagstaff, Ariz.

Seasons of a Navajo (1985). A 57 minute film/video, a PBS production, KAET-TV, Phoenix, Ariz.

Grade Level: Primary

Basic Concepts: Conflict and values

Organizing Generalization: Cultures have different values. Sometimes these values are so different that they are opposite from each other. When values are in conflict, they can cause misunderstandings.

Culture Area: All regions

Time Period: Contemporary

Background: In contemporary American culture, children often receive gifts. Receiving gifts is frequently central at birthday parties, holidays, and as recognition of achievement. In Native American cultures, when children demonstrate achievement or celebrate certain life passages such as receiving a name, dancing for the first time at a powwow, or receiving an award for accomplishment, their family honors them at a giveaway. This ceremony is usually held at a powwow, and the family gives gifts to significant friends as a way of honoring the child. This difference in the giving and receiving of gifts is often difficult for children to understand and is one way to demonstrate to young children how values can differ from one culture to another. It is also preparation for understanding at a later age how differences in Europeans values and traditional Native American values caused conflict, particularly related to ownership. Europeans indicated wealth by how much they accumulated; Native Americans indicated wealth and abundance by what they gave to others.

Objectives:

Knowledge (Content)

Students will:

1. describe how and when children receive gifts in our culture;

2. describe the Native American giveaway; and

3. discuss how customs are handed down from generation to generation.

Skills

Students will:

1. compare how children are honored in traditional Indian cultures and in the dominant culture; and

2. simulate a Native American giveaway.

Values (Organic)

Students will:

appreciate that cultures differ in how they honor children and respect those differences.

Activities:

1. Read a book about birthday parties or a holiday book that discusses children receiving gifts. The teacher can also draw attention to the joy in giving gifts.

2. Invite a Native American person to talk to the children about the giveaway. Some of the best descriptions of this tradition can be found in materials relating to the Potlatch of the Northwest Region.

3. Brainstorm on the occasions children receive gifts in both cultures.

4. Plan a class giveaway ceremony. This provides an opportunity for children to think of what special attributes that each child has that is worthy of honoring. Gifts for the classroom giveaway should be made at school—gifts of service (you can take my place in line)—or make worthy, inexpensive exchanges (used books or toys).

EXTENSIONS

1. Items for the giveaway could be products of art activities

that help children understand Indian cultures.

2. Older students could research the traditional roots of the giveaway in the Potlatch ceremony.

Evaluation:

Children will describe the Native American tradition of giving gifts as a way of honoring children and acknowledge how it is different from the European/Anglo tradition of giving gifts to children.

Materials and Resources:

Bernstein, B., and L. Blair. *Native American Crafts Workshop.* Belmont, Calif.: Pitman Learning, 1982.

The following excerpt from Momaday (1989) is useful in understanding the importance of the giveaway.

> There was a giveaway ceremony, a rite of sharing that occurred in varying ways in tribal cultures across the land. A prominent family of eight or ten members entered the circle. They carried baskets of rich things to give away, beautiful blankets and shawls, German silver and bead work, money and yard goods. They called out the names of well known and highly respected people, those who were most worthy of honors and renown. Mammedaty's name was called out, and he arose and stepped forward. At the same moment a boy came running into the circle, leading a big, black horse. There was suddenly a murmur on the crowd, a wave of sheer excitement and delight. The horse shone like shale; it was dancing, blowing, its flesh rippling; it was perfectly beautiful and full of life. There was white at its eyes; there were bright ribbons and eagle feathers in its mane and there was a beautiful new red blanket spread upon its back.
>
> The horse was presented to Mammedaty, and he graciously returned his thanks, shaking hands with each member of the family. There were nods of approval all around the crowd, and some of the women emitted the shrill, tremolo cries of delight which are peculiar to them. But for all of its color and commotion, it was a moment of great meaning and propriety. All was well with the Kiowa; everything in the world was intact and in place, as it ought to be.

Momaday, N. S. In *The World of the American Indian.* Edited by J.B. Billard. Washington, D.C.: National Geographic Society, 1989.

Grade level: Secondary

Basic Concept: Conflict, discrimination, and religious freedom

Organizing Generalization: All citizens are guaranteed freedom of religion in the first amendment of the Constitution.

Culture Area: Southwest

Time Period: Post-European Contact to 1990

Background: The First Amendment gives all citizens the right to religious choice. Native Americans were made citizens in 1924. There have been many instances in which Native People were denied the basic right to religious choice. From the earliest times, Christian missionaries attempted to convert Native Americans, but usually with little success. After the establishment of the reservations in the 19th century, sacred lands were taken away and ceremonials that had religious significance were forbidden. The struggle to gain religious lands and the right to worship freely has been a political as well as an economic hardship. The Taos Pueblo regained their sacred lake and the rights to free expression of their religion in 1970. Their sacred lands, however, were left in the hands of the Forest Service until the Pueblo petitioned for the land adjoining Blue Lake to be exclusively their property. The Indian Religious Freedom Act has made it possible for Native American Church members to practice their religion, including the use of peyote. These two cases are significant in restoring Indian dignity and self-determination and have importance in terms of the Constitution.

Objectives:

Knowledge (Content)

Students will:

1. locate Taos, New Mexico and Blue Lake on a map;

2. state in their own words the meaning of the First Amendment;

3. distinguish between Constitutional rights and privileges;

4. state the significance of the Indian Religious Freedom Act;

5. discuss the major religious, political, and economic issues that made Blue Lake such a protracted struggle;

6. discuss the social and legal conflicts raised by the Native American Church in expressing its religion; and

7. summarize the relationship between the First Amendment and the rights accorded to or denied Native Americans.

Skills

Students will:

1. use primary source materials; and

2. compare and contrast major issues regarding the religious freedom of Native Americans.

Values (Organic)

Students will:

1. understand that when rights are protected in a pluralistic society, the rights of both the minority and majority are protected;

2. value the right of all people to express religious beliefs; and

3. recognize that when the rights of the minority are denied, the majority also suffers because all rights are then jeopardized.

Activities:

1. Divide students into three groups. Guidesheets will be prepared for each group on the following subjects. One group will read the primary documents that pertain to the return of Blue Lake to the Taos Pueblo. They will prepare a summary of the issues and a time line of the events related to Blue Lake. They will also investigate the economic hardship this litigation put on the Taos Pueblo, including speculation as to what was *not* done with the money that was being used for legal battles.

2. The second group will prepare a summary of the First Amendment to the Constitution and the Indian Religious Freedom Act.

3. The remaining group will research the Native American Church.

4. After class presentations by the three groups, students will discuss the relationship between the First Amendment and rights denied or accorded to Native Americans. A summary paper will be required of each student.

EXTENSIONS

1. Students can do further research into the Native American Church, including talking with Native people. The use of peyote as part of this church's religious expression has caused controversy, particularly in a time of great social concern about the problems resulting from substance abuse. A debate could be presented on whether or not the use of illegal substances in religious services should be reason for an amendment to the Constitution.

2. Another interesting issue for student investigation would be the Ghost Dance. Government fear and subsequent suppression of the Ghost Dance was the cause of the Wounded Knee Massacre in 1890.

3. The following books would be interesting extra reading for some students:

Deloria, V., Jr. *God is Red*. New York: Grosset & Dunlap, 1973.

Fire, J. (Lame Deer), and A. Erdoes. *Lame Deer Seeker of Visions*. New York: Pocket Books, 1972.

Hammerschlag C. *The Dancing Healer*. New York: Harper & Row, 1988.

Evaluation:

1. Can students state the rights afforded in the First Amendment of the Constitution as they apply to both the minority and majority populations, and the significance of the Indian Religious Freedom Act of 1978?

2. After reading documents, can students discuss the value of consulting primary sources?

3. Can students discuss the First Amendment in relation to the request of the Pueblo people for the return of their

lands surrounding Blue Lake and the Indian Religious Freedom Act.

Resources and Materials:

Prucha, F., ed. *Documents of United States Indian Policy*. Lincoln: University of Nebraska Press, 1975.

Moquin, W., and C. Van Doren, eds. *Great Documents in American Indian History*. New York: Praeger Publishers, 1973.

Josephy, A., Jr. *Now That the Buffalo's Gone*. Norman: University of Oklahoma Press, 1986.

CHAPTER SIX
CURRENT ISSUES
FOR NATIVE AMERICANS

They had and have this power for living which our modern world has lost as world-view and self-view, as tradition and institution, as practical philosophy dominating their societies and as an art supreme among all the arts. They had what the world has lost. They have it now. What the world has lost, the world must have again, lest it die. Not many years are left to have or have not; to capture the lost ingredient.

—John Collier 1948

CURRENT ISSUES FOR NATIVE AMERICANS

The major concepts of the *Model for Teaching About Native Americans*, environment, resources, culture, diversity, change, adaptation, and conflict, and discrimination now come together to concentrate on the present and the future of Indian peoples. We admonish the teacher to remember that Native American cultures are part of our history and our future, that they are dynamic cultures that have influenced the past, and are a living, vital presence in the present and future of the United States.

This chapter will explore four major current and future issues for Native Americans and will be guided by the following generalizations:

Past events influence current events. Understanding past events help to enable Native Americans to assume self-determination and the rights and responsibilities of tribal membership and U.S. citizenship.

Rapid social change requires changes in traditional culture and ways of living.

EDUCATION FOR THE FUTURE

Native Americans have been highly successful in educating themselves over the centuries. Their very existence through the years demonstrates the effectiveness of the traditional methods of passing necessary knowledge on to each generation. As years passed, and invasion into their traditional ways of living became common, tribes made efforts to meet the uncontrollable changes that they were experiencing. By the mid-1800s several tribes in the Southeast Region had developed their own systems of modern education. The Choctaw Nation supervised a system of approximately 200 schools and academies. The Cherokee Nation, well-known for its own syllabary (written alphabet) operated schools and were nearly 90 percent literate in Cherokee in the 1850s ("Stuck in the Horizon?" 1989).

By the turn of the 20th century, the Bureau of Indian Affairs (B.I.A.) had either closed down or taken over all Indian-controlled schools. They replaced Indian-controlled education and later B.I.A. day schools on reservations with a system of B.I.A. boarding schools far away from students' reservation homes. By the early 1900s promising B.I.A. reports stated that almost 90 percent of all Native American children were enrolled in one of the various types of schools available, either boarding, day, public, or private.

This statistic is very misleading. The boarding schools, although enrolling high numbers of students in the fall, already had a reputation for harsh physical punishment of students for speaking tribal languages, for practicing tribal customs and wearing tribal dress, for poor teachers and educational standards, for excessive work requirements for students, for overcrowding, and for poor health standards

(Szasz 1984). The result of such poor treatment and inferior educational quality was an extraordinarily high drop-out rate for Indian students.

The day schools on reservations had minimal funding, resulting in the employment of inadequate teachers, overcrowded classrooms, and inappropriate curricula. Public schools gave little, if any, attention to the Indian student. Through the years, the number of students in public schools grew and legislation was provided for the states to receive financial assistance to help meet the special needs of Indian students. This money was often lost in the state and local districts' bureaucracies and little benefit flowed to the students.

The Meriam (1928) Survey first identified these harsh facts that were verified later by another major government report, *Indian Education: A National Tragedy—A National Challenge* (U.S. Congress, Senate, Special Subcommittee on Indian Education of the Committee on Labor and Public Welfare 1969). Dropout rates were too high. The illiteracy rate was staggering. Harsh physical conditions for students existed at some federally-operated schools. Funds had been misappropriated and misused. Tribal identity and culture had been threatened to the point of near extinction. Unfortunately, the Meriam Survey, although receiving a flurry of publicity and prompting some concern, had no major effect on Indian education. For, as the 1969 report (known as the Kennedy report) documents, the same problems were present forty years later. Anglo-Americans had not been successful in educating Native Americans.

In 1970, President Nixon surprised the nation and Congress, when he stated in an address, "It is long past time that the Indian policies of the federal government begin to recognize and build upon the capacities and insights of the Indian People....The time has come to break decisively with the past and to create conditions for a new era in which the Indian future is determined by Indian acts and Indian decisions" ("Stuck in the Horizon?" 1989). This statement expressed the sentiment that set the stage for the modern-day legislation and court decisions that have allowed for change in the education for contemporary Native Americans. That change has taken form slowly and continues to evolve in the present.

The passage of the 1972 Indian Education Act, Title IV of Public Law 92-318, was the first major success for self-determination in education for Native Americans. This legislative act contained provisions for Indian parental and community involvement in public schools with impact aid and other programs for Indians, designated funds for Indian community-operated programs, provided grants for Indian-operated adult education programs, and established a National Advisory Council on Indian Education to strengthen and expand Indian participation and influence in education at both federal and local levels.

This renewed opportunity for participation in educating their young, prompted the development of a plan to allow tribes to contract with the B.I.A. to operate their own schools, beginning with grades K-12 and including community colleges later. Active lobbying and political involvement over the next few years yielded the Indian Self-Determination and Educational Assistance Act of 1975 and the American Indian Higher Education Assistance Act of 1978.

Although these laws appear to be adequate governmental responses to the problems encountered by Native American students, they merely begin to address the inadequate educational status of Native Americans and their continued inability to participate in the decision-making processes that govern their lives.

The U.S. Department of Education statistics in 1980 reveal that Native Americans have the highest dropout rate and they begin to leave school at an earlier age than any other group. In school, they have a greater likelihood than other groups to be labeled as handicapped or learning disabled. This information is alarming. The problem cannot be attributed solely to B.I.A. schools. A recent report ("Stuck in the Horizon?" 1989) reveals that only 10 percent of Indian students throughout the nation attend B.I.A .and Tribal schools (38,000 students). The remaining 370,000 students attend public and private schools on and off reservations.

However, the legacy of the B.I.A. boarding school era remains, even when Indian children are enrolled primarily in public schools. Contemporary Indian parents feel inadequate and often have a minimal education themselves. They have not only been denied full benefits of a quality education, but also have been denied the opportunity to pass on to their children their unique heritage and language.

In 1986, Janine Windy Boy charged that local voting processes systematically kept Crow and Cheyenne people from active participation in governance of the public school system that served their children. In *Windy Boy vs. Big Horn County, Montana*, U.S. District Judge denied access to school and local government because of discriminatory voting practices. Big Horn County, Montana is 46 percent Indian and 52 percent Anglo. Most Anglos live in Hardin, the county seat, and most Crow and Cheyenne live on their respective reservations that comprise almost 90 percent of the county area. Before 1986, only one Indian had ever been on the school board in its entire history. In 1987, after the court ruling, two Indians were elected to the Hardin School Board.

The lessons of the past are evident, as are the problems of the present and the challenges for the future. Margaret Szasz (1984) wrote, "Henceforth direction and leadership in Indian education should come increasingly from the Indians

themselves." The message is a clear statement about the need for and belief in Indian self-determination.

Still, it is too simple and inaccurate to conclude that if Indian people were able to direct the formal education of their children all educational problems would disappear. Indian families and their children share other major concerns of the dominant culture that affect young people and their education—troubled families, substance abuse, under-financed school districts, and a curriculum inappropriate for their social, emotional, and academic needs.

PRESERVATION OF LANGUAGE, CULTURE, AND TRADITION

The Indians must conform to the white man's ways, peaceably if they will, forcibly if they must. They must adjust themselves to their environment, and conform their mode of living substantially to our civilization. This civilization may not be the best possible, but it is the best the Indians can get. They can not escape it, and must either conform to it or be crushed by it.

Thomas Jefferson Morgan (1956) spoke these words shortly after he was named Commissioner of Indian Affairs in 1889. The Native American people were unaware that the United States government intended to obliterate Native American culture. Assimilation was the government policy. To this end, many conscious measures were undertaken in the late 1800s and early 1900s to deny Native Americans the right to speak their own language, worship in their own way, and order their social and political lives. Boarding schools, Christian missionaries, and federal policy during these years played key roles in the plan to destroy native cultures, languages, social orders, and religions.

Simultaneously, the Native American elders of the last century believed strongly that their language, religion, and way of life were viable in the past, in the present, and for the future. Sitting Bull once answered the question of why he would not return to the United States to live on a reservation in this way:

Because I am a red man. If the Great Spirit had desired me to be a white man he would have made me so in the first place. He put in your heart certain wishes and plans, in my heart he put other and different desires. Each man is good in his sight. It is not necessary for eagles to be crows. (Armstrong 1984)

Another leader, Chief Joseph, responded strongly to the question of why missionaries were banned from their reservation:

They will teach us to quarrel about God, as Catholics and Protestants do on the Nez Perce Reservation in Idaho and other places. We do not want to do that. We may quarrel with men sometimes about things on earth, but we never quarrel about the Great Spirit. We do not want to learn that. (Armstrong 1984)

The swift and fierce oppression that overtook Native Americans with the arrival of the European explorers was so devastating, however, that the people were able to respond only to the symptoms of the real change in their lives—that of becoming a subjugated people. This response of defeat is well stated in the Cherokee Memorial to the United States Congress, December 29, 1835:

> In truth, our cause is your own. It is the cause of liberty and justice. It is based on your principles, which we have learned from yourselves....Mental culture, industrial habits, and domestic enjoyments, have succeeded the rudeness of the savage state. We have learned your religion also. We have read your sacred books. Hundreds of our people have embraced your doctrines....On your sentence our fate is suspended....On your kindness, on your humanity, on your compassions, on your benevolence, we rest our hopes.

As a result of this pragmatic acquiescence to defeat, many Native Americans did not undertake efforts to preserve the right to practice tribal religions, speak tribal languages, or maintain ancestral traditions. Consequently, assimilation efforts had significant successes because today a substantial number of Native Americans share the Christian religion, speak only English, and participate primarily in non-Native American cultural activities. When asked of their language or cultural heritage or the present conditions of their tribe, they cannot respond. They have lost their connection to the roots of their people. They did not understand that there was a reason to preserve their history and culture.

The need to preserve the traditions of the past is now clear to Native Americans of all tribes and religious beliefs. Today they join together to teach bilingual programs in many schools, participate in tribal ceremonies and dances, and teach the young about the past and present life of their people. In this way, they take an active role in preserving their heritage.

In addition, Native Americans must actively engage in legislative and court struggles to allow themselves the same right to freedom of religion that is accorded all other citizens of the United States by the First Amendment to the Constitution: "Congress shall make no law respecting an establishment of religion, or prohibiting the free exercise thereof."

By the late 1800s, almost every form of Indian religion was banned on the reservations, and the government prohibited people from speaking native languages in most government and missionary schools. It was not until almost fifty years later that the Indian Reorganization Act, and the Indian Religious Freedom Act returned to Native Americans the freedom to worship their own religion and speak their own languages. The return of these rights was a minor victory in the struggle of Native Americans to be allowed the same rights as other citizens of this nation. This victory took time and persistence.

ACHIEVEMENT OF ADEQUATE PHYSICAL AND SOUND MENTAL HEALTH

Today, when Navajos become ill, they must choose between the white man's physician and their own medicine men. They have to decide which one will cure them. In the past, the Navajo did not believe in the spread of disease and this is still true today for a majority of the people. Illness is caused by disharmony. "There is no word for 'germ' in our language. This makes it hard for the Navajo people to understand sickness" (Cahn 1969).

Statistics reported by the Indian Health Service (*Chart Series*, 1988) reveal that the life expectancy for Native Americans was 71.1 years, as compared to the U.S. white population which was 74.4 years, a difference of only 3.3 years. However, the report further states that the age-adjusted mortality rates for the following causes were considerably higher in 1985 than the U.S. general population.

Alcoholism	321% greater
Tuberculosis	220% greater
Diabetes	139% greater
Accidents	124% greater
Homicide	72% greater
Pneumonia/Influenza	34% greater

Alcoholism has been devastating to Native American people. It has led to the destruction of families, fetal alcohol syndrome, mental illness, suicide, and dysfunctional families. Fetal alcohol syndrome (FAS) carries the detrimental effects directly to the next generation causing a number of conditions including reduction of cognitive reasoning abilities.

Dysfunctional families also pass the negative effects of alcoholism to the next generation by providing poor environments for children. Children respond by assuming traits, roles, or behaviors that are immediately useful, yet handicapping for them in the future.

Suicide rates are extremely high for Native Americans and are symptomatic of deeper personal struggles and stress and feelings of helplessness. Tuberculosis, although causing over 200 percent more deaths among Native Americans than among all other racial groups, has been addressed recently, and is becoming far less frequent than in the past New drugs are primarily responsible for this improvement. The incidence and severity of diabetes and pneumonia have also been reduced with new vaccines and drugs.

Many Native Americans also suffer from ear infections that have lasting effects on hearing. This condition, and others like it, are complicated by inadequate health care. Many must travel long distances to reach Indian Health Service (I.H.S.) facilities and the quality of care available to them is often limited. These same problems were noted twenty years ago by the Indian Health Service and tribal officials. Recent efforts have increased health education training, alcohol and drug treatment programs, prenatal and postnatal care, and other preventive outreach services.

Another major contributor to the poor health condition of Native Americans is substandard housing and sanitary facilities. The I.H.S. reported in 1988 that in 1987 there was an unmet need to serve approximately 21,500 homes. It is estimated that 14 percent of the Native Americans living on reservations do not have adequate water or sewage facilities. These conditions contribute to the already inadequate health care available to them.

Preventive outreach programs that provide education and training have had great success. Sensitive to traditional ways of life and beliefs, the health outreach programs and their personnel interact with Native Americans with respect and understanding. Focused attention is on the cause of a condition rather than on "patching up" the symptoms. For instance, communities and individuals have joined together to sponsor alcohol-free activities and to build support systems to educate and encourage Indian people to reject the patterns of alcoholism.

Native Americans believe that efforts must be undertaken not only to address health problems, but also economic status, social, and environmental factors that continue to contribute to conditions that perpetuate the debilitating health conditions that affect the quality of life for many Native Americans.

DEVELOPMENT OF POLITICAL INFLUENCE AND ECONOMIC SELF-SUFFICIENCY

According to the oral tradition of the Iroquois, a man came among the people as a messenger from the Creator to bring peace and a process to keep peace. The Peacemaker landed on the southeast shore of what is now called Lake Ontario in a great white stone canoe. He called the people together, especially the leaders, and he taught them the Great Law of Peace. He bound five arrows together, representing the Five Nations, and called on the warriors to break the shaft. When no one could accomplish this, he said it signified the strength in their unity. He said the people should act as one mind, body, and heart.

The Peacemaker planted the Great Tree of Peace symbolizing the League of Peace, with a guardian eagle on top. In a pit below the roots he called on all the warriors to cast their weapons of war to be buried. He gave the sacred tobacco to the people to help them communicate with the Creator.

The Peacemaker taught the people that they could handle disputes and adversity without warfare. The society was matrilineal and the clan mothers were given the role and responsibility of selecting the chiefs. Leaders were chosen based upon:

- participatory knowledge of spiritual culture;
- disposition of the Peacemaker;
- genuine feeling for the welfare of old people, women, and children; and

- commitment to protect the Mother Earth for seven generations.

It is said that if a man questioned only once how he could become the chief, he was disqualified for life. Only one who was selfless and did not seek power was felt worthy of the position.

The people of the Five Nations lived a well-organized, political life. They looked to the future seven generations. When considering action or making a decision, their way of life provided for freedom and equal value of individuals and a way to live with each other.

Since this time in history, Native Americans have been stripped of the rights and freedoms that were inherent to their traditional ways of life. They have lost their tribal sovereignty and become dependent people with imposed self-governance systems, with little or no control of the disposition of remaining lands, and a very bleak economic future. Native Americans have a high unemployment rate and a very low socio-economic status.

According to the 1980 Census, there were more Native Americans in urban areas and off reservations than on reservations. The median income was reported to be $13,600, more than $6,000 below the median income for all families. The poverty rate was more than twice the national rate of 12 percent. On reservations, the situation is more grim. Unemployment soars to 50 percent and annual incomes hover between $2,000-$5,000 (U.S. Department of Commerce 1988).

These economic conditions, combined with near cultural annihilation and the loss of sovereignty, prompted Native Americans to launch several bold events to bring attention to and reestablish the true definition of tribal sovereignty. Embittered Indians forcibly occupied the Bureau of Indian Affairs and Alcatraz Prison, and soon after, in 1973, endured a 71-day siege by U.S. marshals, FBI agents, and other police forces at Wounded Knee, South Dakota. These events brought public attention and legal actions that helped to ignite the modern-day struggle to redefine tribal sovereignty.

The Native American Rights Fund (N.A.R.F.) was established in 1970 to assist Native Americans with legal representation regarding the many federal statutes, regulations, and administrative rulings that have become known as "Indian Law" and which govern the lives of Indian people. Through the years, they have defined their mission primarily in terms of the preservation of tribal existence, the protection of tribal natural resources, and the promotion of human rights.

John Echo Hawk, Executive Director of N.A.R.F., believes that the future of Native Americans including the definition of tribal sovereignty and individual Native American rights will be determined in the United States courts and by Native American people. Native American people will be charged with rebuilding and strengthening their culture and language. Current court cases include cases regarding tribal rights to the taxation of businesses within their jurisdiction, treaty rights to fishing, water rights and land control, religious freedom, voting rights, and the right to receive equal benefit from education.

ADAPTATION TO SOCIAL AND TECHNOLOGICAL CHANGE

The wonders of emerging technology have had both positive and negative effects on Native Americans. For example, technology has brought machines and medicines that heal persistent health problems, radio stations that broadcast in native languages to people in remote locations, transportation that diminishes distances between people and makes health care accessible, efficient irrigation systems to carry water to arid areas, long-distance education, and electricity and water to homes. It has also brought pollution and acid rain, dams that destroy lands, and tourists and television that bring the dominant culture into all homes. The effects of technology can have profound social and economic effects as well as the ability to modify or undermine traditional values and ways of living.

The critical issue with rapidly accelerating technology is related to sovereignty and power. Indian people want the right and power to determine how technology can advance their causes and enhance their ways of living. Native Americans have responded to this challenge by concerted efforts to educate Indian teachers, mental health workers, physicians, lawyers, scientists for positions of guardianship and leadership. They want to become directors and intelligent consumers, not victims, of various technologies.

Wallace Black Elk summarizes current issues for Native Americans in the following statement: The issues are human issues of health, dignity, self-respect, freedom, and self-determination within the context of the sacred road, the red road.

> Real soon, now, this is a turning point. The hoop, the sacred hoop was broken here at Wounded Knee, and it will come back again. The stake here that represents the tree of life, the tree will bloom, it will flower again, and all the people will rejoin and come back to the sacred road, the red road.
>
> —Wallace Black Elk, Wounded Knee, 1973
> (Lincoln and Slagle 1987)

References

Armstrong, V.I., ed. *I Have Spoken: American History Through the Voices of the Indians.* Athens, Ohio: Swallow Press, 1984.

Begley, S., and T. Namuth. "Crazy Horse Rides Again." *Newsweek,* February 1988, 47.

Cahn, E.S., ed. *Our Brother's Keeper: The Indian in White America.* New York: New Community Press, 1969.

Collins, J. *Indians of the Americas.* New York: The New American Library, 1948.

Flowers, B., ed. *Bill Moyers: A World of Ideas.* New York: Doubleday, 1989.

Lincoln K., with A. L. Slagle. *The Good Red Road.* San Francisco, Calif.: Harper and Row, 1987.

Matthiessen, P. *In the Spirit of Crazy Horse.* New York: Viking, 1983.

Meriam, L., et al. *The Problem of Indian Administration.* Baltimore, Md.: The Brookings Institution, 1928.

Morgan, T. J. *A Sketch of the Development of the Bureau of Indian Affairs and of Indian Policy.* Washington, D.C.: Bureau of Indian Affairs, 1956.

"Stuck in the Horizon?" *Education Week,* August 2, 1989.

Szasz, M. C. *Education and the American Indian: The Road to Self-Determination.* Albuquerque: University of New Mexico Press, 1984.

U.S. Congress, Senate Special Subcommittee on Indian Education of the Committee on Labor and Public Welfare. *Indian Education: A National Tragedy—A National Challenge.* Senate Report No. 91-501. Washington, D.C.: U.S. Government Printing Office, 1969.

U.S. Department of Commerce. *We, The First Americans.* Washington, D.C.: Bureau of the Census, 1988.

U.S. Department of Health and Human Services. *Chart Series.* Washington, D.C.: Indian Health Service, 1988.

Lesson Plans

Grade Level: Intermediate

Basic Concepts: Separation and assimilation

Organizing Generalization: The value of assimilation of their minority culture into the dominant culture remains an issue for Native Americans.

Culture Area: General

Time Period: Contemporary

Background: For over one hundred years, the reservation has been home to many Native Americans. Because of the impoverishment of the reservations, some are questioning their viability. The critics point to the poor health, alcoholism, unemployment, and hopelessness of reservation life as reasons to eliminate them and encourage the assimilation of Native people into the dominant culture. Others support the maintenance of reservations because they are the home of Indian culture to Native Americans, whether or not they live on reservations.

Objectives:

Knowledge (Content)

Students will:

1. locate the reservations mentioned in the attached editorial;

2. list the arguments for and against the maintenance of reservations, as presented in the editorial at the end of this lesson plan;

3. describe current reservation life in South Dakota; and

4. describe the current economic and political life of urban Indian people.

Skills

Students will:

1. use atlases to determine the location and size of reservations in South Dakota;

2. identify the perspective of the author of the editorial;

3. use research skills to compile data on the current economic and health-related problems of urban and reservation Indian people;

4. compare economic and health statistics of Native Americans and people of the dominant culture; and

5. interview local Native American people on their opinions regarding the elimination of reservations.

Values (Organic)

Students will:

1. begin to understand what the author means by the concept of "home";

2. recognize that there are strong arguments for both sides of this issue; and

3. acknowledge that it is important to be informed when making a complex, and far-reaching decision and that there are long-term consequences for decisions of this kind.

Activities:

1. In groups of three, students will (a) read the editorial and identify the perspective of the author, (b) list the arguments for the elimination of reservations, (c) list the arguments against the elimination of the reservations, and (d) draw a map of South Dakota, locating the state among its neighbors, the reservations, the major land forms, and water bodies.

2. Resource materials should be available so that student groups can determine current statistics about the economic and health status of Native Americans and the dominant culture.

3. Invite local Native American people to present their views on the topic to the class. Class members should prepare interview questions in advance for the guest speaker.

4. As a class, discuss the arguments for and against elimination of the reservation, using the variety of information gathered. Encourage *vigorous* discussion of *both* perspectives. Make large charts summarizing the major arguments for both positions.

5. Using the information collected, each student will take a position in writing on the issue. Any position, logically presented, is acceptable.

EXTENSIONS

1. Students can write letters to the author of the editorial, or to legislators or leaders in their own states, expressing their reasoned opinions.

2. Schedule a debate on the topic.

3. Students can explore the idea of "home" in their lives and the lives of other American minority groups. This topic would lend itself to creative expression (e.g., posters, songs, or poetry).

4. Ask students to write an essay in response to the following quotation by Louise Erdrich and Michael Dorris, two Native American authors and scholars.

I don't think people who are living on reservations or the half of American Indians who are urban Indians think of reservations as traps. They are places where the culture is strongest, where the family is, where the roots are—where the language is spoken—and where the people around you understand you, and you understand them. Even if you are of mixed background, you feel comfortable on a reservation. (Flowers 1989)

Evaluation:

Based upon their research and exploration of the issues related to the topic, students will make an informed decision as to whether or not Indian reservations should be eliminated.

Materials and Resources:

Flowers, B., ed. *Bill Moyers: A World of Ideas.* New York: Doubleday, 1989.

Basic research materials.

THE END OF RESERVATIONS?

Joseph H. Cash, University of South Dakota

United Tribes News, June, 1989 (adapted)

It is 1989 and it is the centennial of the State of South Dakota. It is also the centennial of the Agreement of 1889 that broke up the great Sioux reservation into smaller reservations. Some people say that these small reservations have outlived their usefulness and are not serving the Indian people well. They say that the reservations should be broken up and done away with. However, some whites and Indians disagree.

It is difficult to defend many parts of the West River Reservations. Without outside help, there is no way that they can support the people that live there. Even with outside help, unemployment rates are from 70-90 percent. The government comes through with enough to keep people from actually starving but with little more.

This poverty causes problems. The crime rate on the reservations is extremely high and is higher than other counties and towns. Violence is common. Alcoholism is also common and is the cause of much of the crime. The family, so important to the Indian people, seems to be crumbling. Yet, the people cling to the reservations and many wonder why.

One of the reasons is that the reservation is the homeland. It is all that is left of two continents once completely owned by Indian people. The people must survive here. In addition, here are the huge families that are so important to Indians. The aunts, uncles, cousins, grandparents and other relatives form a safe place around the individual. This place is what (the Indian people need) to function and to survive. Where else but (on) a reservation can it be kept?

The reservation is also a great cultural center. It is here that the language is preserved. It is here that Indian religion lives on. It is here that the ceremonies and the dances continue. With no reservation many of these things would stop. They would become part of the past, not the present.

The reservation is also a place where (Indians) can be what (they want) to be. If a person should choose to use the reservation as a springboard toward education and the entrance to the larger society, he (or she) can certainly do so. If, on the other hand, it is possible for a person to stay and live with traditional Indian life and values. The reservation is for all Indian lifestyles.

Will we lose the reservation? It is possible, but if we do, we will lose a great deal, whether we are Indian or white. Certainly the weaknesses of tribal government can be overcome. Better people can run for office and (we hope will) be elected. Certain changes can take place in government. Tribal law enforcement can be upgraded. Indian students who are becoming lawyers should bring positive change. Indian health can improve. Indeed, it has improved quite a lot in the last twenty years.

This leaves us with employment, which is the toughest of all the problems to solve. It is likely that more people will have to leave the reservation to find jobs. Still, the reservation should be there for them to visit or to (which they can) retire. A healthier reservation can help the Indian people and it can help the state of South Dakota which cannot afford to have the present situation. We should not end the reservation, but improve it and make it a better thing for all.

Grade Level: Secondary

Basic Concepts: Conflict and discrimination

Organizing Generalization: Discrimination can be present, even under the authority of the law.

Culture Area: Plains

Time Period: Contemporary

Background: As a result of the protests of the American Indian Movement (A.I.M.) at Wounded Knee, South Dakota in the early 1970s, violence erupted and a seventy-one day standoff took place between the F.B.I. and the A.I.M. followers. In 1975, the F.B.I. returned to a still-troubled situation at the Pine Ridge Reservation. In a shootout with a small group of people on the reservation, two F.B.I. agents were killed. Leonard Peltier was apprehended and convicted of the crime. He is currently serving two consecutive life terms for those murders, although he claims his innocence. Not only has there been Native American protest, but there has been extensive international protest of the manner in which the trial was conducted. The courts refuse to grant a new trial to Peltier.

Objectives:

Knowledge (Content)

Students will:

1. become familiar with the political background of the A.I.M. movement and its place in the protest movements of the 1970s;

2. place these historical events within the context of the continuing struggle of Native Americans with the jurisdiction of the Federal Government; and

3. come to personal conclusions as to whether justice has been served in this case.

Skills

Students will:

1. use research skills while gaining pertinent information from a variety of perspectives;

2. distinguish between fact and opinion in reading and

discussing the different points of view on this case;

3. prepare cogent arguments for their point of view when discussing whether a new trial should be held; and

4. listen to each others' positions and distinguish between arguments based on fact and those based on values.

Values (Organic)

Students will:

1. distinguish between justice and legality and determine which is being served in this case;

2. listen to the opinions of others with respect; and

3. discuss an issue that involves the concepts of law and order and justice. This exercise will be useful in raising cognitive conflict and promoting moral reasoning ability.

Activities:

1. Review appropriate sources of information for research on this case. If possible, locate an A.I.M. member and an attorney as guest speakers in the classroom.

2. The entire class will brainstorm possible positions to the question of retrial of Peltier.

3. In teams of approximately three members, students will prepare briefs to state clearly the background of the case. These briefs will be used as the basis upon which students will develop their personal position.

4. Students will prepare and present position papers regarding whether Peltier should be granted a new trial.

5. The class may not come to consensus on this issue. This is a good time to discuss the organizing generalization.

EXTENSIONS

1. Students can write a letter to Amnesty International, which has taken a stand with regard to this case, or to the Federal Courts to state their opinion regarding a new trial. These opinions should be supported with the facts from their research, the briefs, and class discussion.

2. Discuss whether or not an injustice can be perpetrated without a serious effect on the entire society.

Evaluation:

Students will:

1. describe the difference between legality and justice;

2. make a rational decision with regard to a value-laden problem and express it;

3. treat the opinions of others with respect; and

4. take personal action, by writing a letter or by deciding not to take a public stand at this time. Letters may be in support or opposition to a new trial for Peltier.

Materials and Resources:

Begley, S., and T. Namuth. "Crazy Horse Rises Again." *Newsweek,* February 1, 1988, 47.

Matthiessen, P. *In the Spirit of Crazy Horse.* New York: Viking, 1983.

This is a very controversial book, described as being a one-sided view of people and events. Teachers should consult other resources as well.

CHAPTER SEVEN
RESOURCES FOR TEACHERS AND STUDENTS

I would caution readers and students of American Indian life and culture to remember that Indian America does not in any sense function in the same ways or from the same assumptions that western systems do. Unless and until that fact is clearly acknowledged, it is virtually impossible to make much sense out of the voluminous materials available concerning American Indians.

—Paula Gunn Allen (1986)

RESOURCES FOR TEACHERS AND STUDENTS

CRITERIA FOR EVALUATING EDUCATIONAL MATERIALS

This principle must be stated clearly and in a straightforward manner. The appropriateness and quality of materials used in the classroom depends on the knowledge, understanding, and sensitivity of the classroom teacher. There is an overwhelming profusion of educational materials about Native Americans—books, curriculum guides, activity books, films, filmstrips, videos, maps, puzzles, posters, and games. Unlike the scarcity of materials about other cultural and ethnic groups, shelves and catalogs offer a tempting array of books and curriculum materials about Native Americans. At any age or grade level and from preschool toys to specialized, academic materials for adult scholars, educational materials proliferate. In fact, in 1981, it was estimated that there were more than 6,000 books that were theoretically available for purchase. That figure does not include the mass of materials now out of print, but still available in libraries.

As a consequence, it is impossible to construct a list of "acceptable" materials; teachers are required to become sophisticated and discriminating consumers. They must be able to review critically existing and recent materials, ask probing and difficult questions, refuse the popular, adapt the unsuitable, and be willing, through the selection of curriculum materials, to teach students to appreciate and respect a culture so different from their own. It is undoubtedly as important to teach our youth to detect inaccuracy, ethnocentricity, historical bias, prejudice, and authenticity, as it is to teach them specific social science content.

Some of the major problems that a teacher must confront are:

1. *Authorship, perspective, historical bias*

Early works about Native Americans were written by Anglo-European explorers or anthropologists. This clearly indicates that "too frequently the information is a porthole view about a people, but not from the perspective of the people described" (Council on Interracial Books for Children 1980). With regard to literature, Diane Hoeveler (1988) reminds us "that most Indian writings produced before 1968 are what is known as 'told to' autobiographies. Those Indians who did write themselves were almost solely converts to Christianity, products of Christian educations, writing for the explicit purpose of converting other Indians." Teachers are cautioned to know the experience and perspective of the creators of any curriculum materials.

2. *Cultural accuracy and voice*

Mary Gloyne Byler (1973) states, "While non-Indian authors may produce well-written and entertaining children's books featuring American Indians, there is little in their stories that tells us much about American Indians. We do learn what non-Indians imagine Indians to be, or think they should be."

Anna Stensland (1979) also points out when the teacher selects literature by or about Native Americans for classroom use that it is important to consider all of the criteria that apply to the selection of any good literature. If the teacher is non-Indian it is difficult to ascertain whether the story is true to the Indian way. She urges that teachers consult bibliographies developed by Indian organizations or depend on reviews by Indian scholars. This advice remains useful.

With an increase in Indian authors, both traditional and contemporary in perspective, it should become easier to locate textbooks and other materials that present an Indian voice and cultural accuracy.

3. *Methods of inclusion*

A very interesting and helpful way to analyze how Native Americans are included in curriculum materials is to consider that inclusion of minority people is usually as "greats," as "contributors," and as "protestors." Inclusion as such usually focuses on great men, sometimes interesting women, and spot appearances, thus ignoring the average citizens who have served a primary role in creating and shaping political, social, and economic events throughout history, or those who go about their daily lives as citizens, with human joys and human problems. It is also an easy way to ignore dealing with the causes and possible solutions to persisting social, economic, and political problems faced by many minorities.

Another dimension to inclusion is exclusion. For example, in one major history text the prologue states, "Discovering America is a way of discovering ourselves. This is a book about us" (Boorstin and Kelley 1986, 1). Then a few pages later, in the introductory chapter of a lengthy book of 855 pages, less than one page is devoted to "North American Indians." The message of exclusion is often clear.

4. *Assumptions*

Finally, implicit in all textbooks is the assumption that the European settlers and the United States government had the moral and legal right to dominate a people and a land. Excuses are often cursory and flimsy. For example, "In the 1850s (although they never planned it that way) white men, women, and children began to move into these areas once reserved for Indians (Boorstin and Kelley 1986, 322). Beware of basic assumptions.

Textbooks present a serious problem, for they are usually in classrooms for three to seven years. They not only influence one entire group of students but they continue to do so—year after year. It seems incumbent upon educators to be especially vigilant in textbook selection. It is, of course, possible for good teachers to make effective use of inadequate textbooks. However, the marketplace speaks, and teachers can demand textbooks that are accurate and free of stereotyping.

Even when teachers are supplied with guidelines for literature that identify the literary contributions deemed appropriate for teaching about specific ethnic or cultural groups, the teacher must remain vigilant. This is not as easy as it might appear. One author, Seale (1981) suggests that we are, in general, dealing with a flawed genre; we do not have as much to work with as it may appear. The Council on Interracial Books for Children (1980) proposes that teachers ask the following questions when selecting student textbooks and using literature in the classroom.

I. CHARACTERIZATION

A. Are characters stereotyped in ways listed below?

Male Stereotypes
savage, bloodthirsty "native"
stoic, loyal follower
hunter, tracker
noble child of nature
wise old chief
evil medicine man
brave boy endowed by nature with special "Indian" qualities

Female Stereotypes
heavyset, workhorse "squaw"
"Indian princess" (depicted with European features and often in love with a white man for whom she is willing to sacrifice her life)
drunken comic

Occupational Stereotypes
hunters
cattle thieves
warriors
unemployed loafers
craftspeople

B. Does the story line create negative characterization of Native peoples?

C. Do white perspectives characterize the Native American characters negatively?

II. LANGUAGE AND TERMINOLOGY

A. Are full names of Native American characters given? It is best to present phonetically the correct Indian name as it is pronounced in its own particular native language.

B. Do Native Americans grunt, whoop, or "how" their way through the textbook?

C. Is exotic or stilted speech used? (e.g., many moons ago, me come)?

D. Are derogatory words such as buck, squaw, papoose, used instead of man, woman, and baby?

E. Are "loaded words" used (e.g., savage, stealthy, skulking, stoic, roaming, massacre, heathen, primitive, painted, naked, wild, furtive)?

F. Are Native Americans compared to animals (e.g., "untamed as a wolf")?

G. Are Native peoples labeled as either "friendly" or "unfriendly?"

III. HISTORICAL ACCURACY

A. Are the sites, dates, actions, and statements about treaties presented accurately and is the Native perspective included?

B. If the story takes place in the past, is it accurate and particular to one of the hundreds of differing native cultures in existence at the time?

C. Are achievements of Native Americans in context of the benefits accruing to their own societies or in terms of their benefits to white people?

D. Are the contributions of Native nations to U.S. law, medicine, philosophy, sports, and literature indicated?

E. Is resistance by Native peoples to invasion, treaty breaking, and acculturation described, omitted, or glossed over?

F. If Native American heroes are described, are those who were hostile to whites also included? Or are the heroes selected only those known to be friendly and helpful to whites (e.g., Pocahontas and Squanto)?

IV. CULTURAL AUTHENTICITY

A. Does the text present Native cultures from a Eurocentric perspective? Or is the culture respectfully presented in terms of the values and belief systems that undergird it?

B. Are completely different Native cultures, ways of life, clothing, and homes jumbled into one "Indian" stereotype of feathered headdresses, tipis, and peace pipes? Or does the textbook reflect the fact that the hundreds of Native cultures were, and are, enormously diverse?

C. When the text depicts peace pipes, eagle feathers, dances, and ceremonies, are they shown as exotica or is their religious significance and cultural usage accurately portrayed?

V. ILLUSTRATIONS

A. Are all Native peoples of the past identified by feathers and tipis or are the varied clothing, hairstyles, and homes accurate for the particular nation and historical period illustrated?

B. Are Native people of the present depicted as wearing feathers, braids, or beads or are they illustrated in the many hairstyles and clothes they actually wear (which are generally the same type of contemporary clothing worn by non-Native people)?

C. Is an unreal red tone used to show skin color?

D. Do offensive images appear of non-Native American children wearing feathers and "playing Indian?" A person of any race can play a professional role such as police officer, a clown, or a cowboy or cowgirl. Being an Indian is not a profession, but a condition of being. To let children think that feathers or tomahawks symbolize "Indianhood" is to encourage stereotyping and dehumanizing Native peoples.

The Council for Interracial Books for Children (1980) provides a checklist evaluating the accuracy of information related to Native Americans which is presented in secondary history textbooks. The following twenty-six informational statements are used as a basis for analyzing the quality of a particular textbook or other resource materials as to perspective, inclusion, accuracy, and adequacy of information presented. Teachers are to rate the statements as to (1) incorrect information, (2) no information, (3) omits this period, (4) limited information, and (5) full information. Statements marked with an asterisk (*) are strong statements, made when this guide was written in 1980; they would need to be modified to make them more accurate for 1990.

ANALYZING STATEMENTS

1. Native Americans are the original inhabitants of North America.

2. Pre-Columbian Native American societies reflected great diversity and complexity.

3. The myth of "discovery" is blatantly Eurocentric.

4. At least ten to twelve million Native peoples may have lived in what later became the United States.

5. "Advanced culture" is an ethnocentric concept and does not explain or justify European conquest.

6. War and violence were not characteristics of Indian nations.

7. Native American technology and knowledge were achievements in their own right.

8. Missionary activities were an integral part of European conquest.

9. Native nations made alliances with European nations for their own strategic purposes.

10. Conflicting European and colonial economic interests in Native lands helped trigger the U.S. revolution.

11. Native nations fought the invaders to maintain their communities and lands.

12. Land has a special significance to Native Americans and has been the central issue of conflict with the United States.

13. It is Eurocentric to categorize Native peoples as either "friendly" or "unfriendly."

14. United States policies toward Native Americans reflect many political and economic factors within U.S. society.

15. Textbook terminology is Eurocentric, ignoring Native American presence and perspectives.

16. Legally binding treaties are central to the relations between Indian nations and the United States.

17. The 1881 Dawes Act resulted in the loss of three-quarters of the remaining land of Native Americans.

18. The Citizenship Act of 1924 was not a benevolent action.

19. The Reorganization Act of 1934 heightened Native American alienation and powerlessness.

20. The termination policy of the 1950s resulted in the loss of more land and the abrogation of treaties.

*21. The B.I.A. is a corrupt and inefficient bureaucracy controlling the affairs of one million people.

*22. Oppressive conditions led to a proportionately lower population increase for Native Americans.

23. Reservations represent a paradox for Native Americans.

24. Treaty rights, sovereignty, self-determination, and the return of land are the major goals of Native peoples.

25. The struggle to maintain land continues today.

26. There is a relationship between the past experiences and the present reality of Native Americans.

If in doubt, it is best to use only books written by Native authors. At least, you will have the thought and opinion of a Native person. Unless you are in a position to explain, or elaborate on, a flawed work, it is really better to have nothing than to hand a child a book that will, if she/he is Native, damage her/his self-image, or if the reader is white, reinforce the feelings of superiority and contempt for others that have poisoned human relationships in this country for so long. (Doris Seale, 1981)

RESOURCES FOR TEACHERS

Non-Fiction

Recognizing then that teachers have a multitude of books about Native Americans to choose from in order to increase their own understanding, and that each of us, depending on personal interest, academic background, grade level or subject area taught, and geographic location, has favorite authors and well-used books, the following selections are offered as general, basic, and good introductions to the study of Native Americans. They represent books we have found to be useful and would suggest as a *beginning* to a professional collection.

Armstrong, V.I. *I Have Spoken: American History Through the Voices of the Indians*. Athens, Ohio: Swallow Press, 1984.

A collection of American Indian oratory from the 17th to the

20th century. This invaluable collection of speeches and other wrtings is the Indians' story told with wit, beauty, and integrity. It presents a much needed Indian perspective on American history.

Billard, J.B., ed. *The World of the American Indian*. Washington, D.C: National Geographic Society, 1989.

A broad overview provided with the particular imprint of the National Geographic Society. With contributions of Native Americans, there is a particular poetic beauty as a theme of this book.

Brandon, W. *The American Heritage Book of Indians*. New York: American Heritage, 1961.

A classic of American Indian history that balances a comprehensive narrative and provides an overview of various tribes from the dawn of civilization through the reservation period with over 450 illustrations.

Brown, D. *Bury My Heart at Wounded Knee*. New York: Pocket Books, 1970.

One of the most commonly used and quoted protest books written by a Native American during the time of political protest and national interest in the freedom and sovereignty of Indian peoples.

Deloria, V., Jr. *God is Red*. New York: Grosset and Dunlap, 1973.

A thought-provoking discussion of the current religious climate on the American continent and its relationship to Christianity and the traditional American Indian religions.

Deloria, V., Jr. *Custer Died for Your Sins: An Indian Manifesto*. Norman: University of Oklahoma Press, 1988.

The message of the book is that Indians are being overrun by the ignorance and the mistaken, misdirected efforts of those who would help them. Deloria discusses missionaries, anthropologists, legal policies, and racial discrimination.

Deloria, V., Jr., and C. M. Lytle. *American Indian, American Justice*. Austin: University of Texas Press, 1984.

A good source for those concerned with the contemporary American Indian. It explores the complexity of legal and political rights in understandable language. The authors cite specific examples to illustrate how tribes have adapted their customs and institutions to meet the demands of the modern world.

Erdoes, R., and A. Ortiz, eds. *American Indian Myths and Legends*. New York: Pantheon, 1984.

This comprehensive collection of 166 myths and legends is composed of three sections: (1) stories collected by the authors over a period of 25 years, (2) classic accounts in their original form, and (3) tales retold in an authentic and readable form. Although written for adult readers, these myths and legends can be used at all grade levels to enrich the social studies curriculum.

Fire, J. (Lame Deer), and A. Erdoes. *Lame Deer: Seeker of Visions*. New York: Pocket Books, 1972.

A personal favorite that is useful in gaining insight and understanding into Native American spirituality and the Indian experience.

Josephy, A.M., Jr. *Now That the Buffalo's Gone*. Norman: University of Oklahoma Press, 1986.

Addresses, with painstaking research, the major issues facing American Indians today.

Josephy, A.M., Jr. *The Indian Heritage of America*. New York: Knopf, 1968.

Josephy discusses the history, archeology, and ethnology of all the major Indian cultures. He reconstructs Indian societies as they were before the Europeans, and presents a true portrait of Indians as they were in the distant past and when the book was printed.

Kopper, P. *The Smithsonian Book of North American Indians before the Coming of the Europeans*. New York: Smithsonian Books, 1986.

An invaluable book, abundant with illustrations, that presents a thorough picture of what is known about Indian peoples before the Europeans. It discusses the quest for knowledge about these aboriginal people and takes care to suggest the tentativeness of our knowledge.

Lincoln, K. *Native American Renaissance*. Berkeley: University of California Press, 1983.

Teachers who are avid readers or who interested in or use Native American literature will find this book fascinating reading and very useful in understanding this particular genre.

Maxwell, J.A. ed. *America's Fascinating Indian Heritage*. Pleasantville, N.Y.: The Reader's Digest Association, 1987.

An overview of traditional Indian cultures, replete with drawings, maps, and pictures. A brief section describes the renaissance of Native people. An appendix lists museums, reconstructed villages, and archaeological sites open to the public.

McLuhan, T.C. *Touch the Earth*. New York: Simon and Schuster, 1971.

This beautiful book, comprised of the words of speeches and writings by Indian people, is a chronicle of the loss of a way of life. Many selections were futile efforts to offer ideas to the white man.

Ortiz, A., ed. *Earth Power Coming*. Tsaile, Ariz.: Navajo Community College Press, 1983.

A valuable collection of short fiction written by thirty Native American authors. Most of the fiction is grounded in the Indian oral tradition.

Spicer, E.H. *A Short History of the Indians of the United States.* Malabar, Fla.: Robert E. Krieger Publishing, 1983.

Spicer strives to present perspectives on Indian history that differ from the perspective of the dominant society. An impressive section includes documents regarding Indian history as seen by Indians, white policies and viewpoint, and Indian prophets and spokesmen.

Spicer, E.H. *The American Indians.* Cambridge, Mass.: Belknap Press of Harvard University Press, 1980.

An easy-to-read and comprehensive overview that is an extremely valuable resource to teachers in understanding the high degree of diversity in American Indian people.

Waldman, C. *Atlas of the North American Indian.* New York: Facts on File, 1985.

This book has recently gone out of print. However, it is such a gold mine of invaluable information, teachers are urged to find a copy quickly. The maps are clear and summarize a wide variety of information in a succinct visual image. The text is straight-forward and very readable.

MAGAZINES—NEWSLETTERS— JOURNALS

Akwesasne Notes (Official publication of the Mohawk Nation)
Rooseveltown, NY 13683-0196
(518) 358-9531

Daybreak Star Reader
United Indians of all Tribes
Daybreak Star Arts Center -Discovery Park
P.O. Box 99100
Seattle, WA 98199
(206) 285-4425

Native Peoples
1833 North Third St.
Phoenix, AZ 95004-1502

United Tribes News
3315 University Drive
Bismarck, ND 58504
(701) 255-3285 x 293

Winds of Change
1985 14th Street, Suite 1224
Boulder, CO 80302

ORGANIZATIONS

American Indian Historical Society
1451 Masonic Avenue
San Francisco, CA 94117

Council on Interracial Books for Children
1841 Broadway

Room 500
New York, NY 10023
(212) 757-5339

Department of the Interior
18th & C Streets, N.W.
Washington, DC 20240
(202) 343-5815

Native American Rights Fund
1506 Broadway
Boulder, CO 80302
(303) 477-8760

National Native American Cooperative
P.O. Box 5000
San Carlos, AZ 85550-0301
(602) 244-8244

Newberry Library Center for the History of the American Indian
60 West Walton Street
Chicago, IL 60610
(312) 943-9090

The Smithsonian Institution
Public Affairs Office
Department of Anthropology
Stop Code 112
Washington, DC 20560
(202) 357-1592

RESOURCES FOR STUDENTS

This section has been difficult to compile. Interestingly enough, many books and most reviews were written in the 1960s and 1970s. Another complication has been that it is difficult to ascertain which authors are Native people. Some of the following books are old, personal favorites and undoubtedly some are flawed, according to the standards we have listed above. Teachers can use the flaws, however, as an opportunity to heighten students' awareness and increase learning.

A further difficulty is that books that have been strongly recommended by Indian people often are not readily available from the sources known to most teachers and consequently are difficult to obtain. Finally, there are locally produced books and materials (e.g., materials provided or produced by local and state historical societies and books used in Indian education programs) that are not known or easily accessible to the general population.

FICTION/POETRY/PROSE— ELEMENTARY AND MIDDLE SCHOOL

Amon, A. *The Earth Is Sore: Native Americans On Nature.* New York: Atheneum, 1981.

Baylor, B. *Before You Came This Way.* New York: E. P. Dutton, 1969.

Books by Byrd Baylor are particularly recommended.

Bierhorst, J., ed. *In the Trail of the Wind: American Indian Poems and Ritual Orations*. New York: Farrar, Straus, & Giroux, 1971.

Books by John Bierhorst are particularly recommended.

Carter, F. *The Education of Little Tree*. New York: Delacorte, 1976.

Eastman, C. *Indian Boyhood*. New York: Dover, 1971.

Jeffery, D. *Geronimo*. Milwaukee, Wisc.: Raintree, 1990.

This book is part of a series, American Indian Stories, published by Raintree Press. The books in this series are written with the assistance of Native People and scholars in the field and are highly recommended.

Goble, P. *The Gift of the Sacred Dog*. New York: Bradbury Press, 1980.

Books by Paul Goble are particularly recommended.

Hale, J.C. *The Owl's Song*. New York: Avon, 1976.

Haviland, V., ed. *North American Legends*. New York, 1979.

Hillerman, T. *The Boy Who Made Dragonfly*. Albuquerque: University of New Mexico Press, 1988.

McDermott, G. *Arrow to the Sun*. New York: Penguin, 1977.

Miles, M. *Annie and the Old One*. Boston, Mass.: Little Brown, 1971.

Morrow, M.F. *Sarah Winnemucca*. Milwaukee, Wisc.: Raintree, 1990.

Part of the Raintree series, American Indian Stories.

O'Dell, S. *Island of the Blue Dolphins*. New York: Dell, 1960.

O'Dell, S. *Sing Down the Moon*. New York: Dell, 1970.

Yue, C. *The Pueblo*. Boston, Mass.: Houghton-Mifflin, 1986.

Books written by Charlotte and David Yue are strongly recommended.

FICTION/POETRY/PROSE—ADULTS & HIGH SCHOOL

Bennett, K. *Kaibah: Recollections of a Navajo Girlhood*. Los Angeles: Westernlore Press, 1964.

Craven, M. *I Heard the Owl Call My Name*. New York: Dell, 1973.

Erdrich, L. *Love Medicine*. New York: Bantam, 1984.

Highwater, J. *Anpao: An American Indian Odyssey*. Philadelphia, Pa.: Lippincott, 1977.

Highwater, J. *Ceremony of Innocence*. New York: Harper, 1985.

Books by Jamaka Highwater have been praised and negatively criticized by Native People.

Hillerman, T. *A Thief of Time*. New York: Harper & Row, 1988.

Books written by Tony Hillerman are excellent, entertaining mystery novels that subtly expose the reader to Navajo culture.

Hobson, G., ed. *The Remembered Earth: An Anthology of Contemporary Native American Literature*. Albuqerque: University of New Mexico Press, 1981.

LaFlesche, F. *The Middle Five: Indian Schoolboys of the Omaha Tribe*. Madison: University of Wisconsin Press, 1963.

McNickle, D. *The Surrounded*. Albuquerque: University of New Mexico Press, 1978.

McNickle, D. *Wind from an Enemy Sky*. New York: Harper & Row, 1978.

Milton, J.R., ed. *The American Indian Speaks*. Vermillion: University of South Dakota Press, 1970.

Mitchell, E.B. *Miracle Hill: The Story of a Navaho Boy*. Norman: University of Oklahoma Press, 1967.

Momaday, N.S. *The House Made of Dawn*. New York: Harper and Row, 1969.

Momaday, N.S. *The Names: A Memoir*. New York: Harper and Row, 1976.

N. Scott Momaday is a prolific and respected Indian author. His books are highly recommended.

Neihardt, J. G. *Black Elk Speaks: Being the Life Story of a Holy Man of the Ogalala Sioux*. New York: Pocket Books, 1972.

Silko, L.M. *Ceremony*. New York: Signet, 1977.

Leslie Marmon Silko is a contemporary Indian author. Her books are highly recommended.

Storm, H. *Seven Arrows*. New York: Harper and Row, 1972.

This books has been praised and negatively criticized by Native People.

Velie, A.R., ed. *American Indian Literature. An Anthology*. Norman: University of Oklahoma Press, 1982.

Waters, F. *The Man Who Killed the Deer*. New York: Pocket Books, 1971.

Welch, J. *The Death of Jim Loney*. New York: Harper & Row, 1979.

Welch, J. *Winter in the Blood*. New York: Harper & Row, 1974.

James Welch is a respected, contemporary Indian author. His books are highly recommended.

NON-FICTION—STUDENT

Caduto, J.J., and J. Bruchac. *Keepers of the Earth: Native American Stories and Environmental Activities for Children*. Golden, Colo.: Fulcrum, 1988.

Harlan, J. *American Indians Today*. New York: Franklin Watts, 1987.

Hirschfelder, A. *Happily May I Walk*. New York: Charles Scribner's Sons, 1986.

Weatherford, J.M. *Indian Givers: How the Indians of the Americas Transformed the World*. New York: Crown, 1988.

The authors would be honored if teachers would send us the names of books and materials they have used and their reviews of these resources.

References that were particularly useful in writing this chapter are:

Council on Interracial Books for Children. *Guidelines for Selecting Bias-free Textbooks and Story Books*. New York: Council on Interracial Books for Children, 1980.

Hirschfelder, A.B. *American Indian Stereotypes in the World of Children: A Reader and Bibliography*. Metuchen, N.J.: Scarecrow Press, 1982.

References

Allen, P.G. *The Sacred Hoop*. Boston, Mass.: Beacon Press, 1986.

Boorstin, D. J., and B. M. Kelley. *A History of the United States*. Lexington, Mass.: Ginn, 1986.

Byler, M. G. *American Indian Authors for Young Readers*. New York: Association on Indian Affairs, 1973.

Council on Interracial Books for Children. *Guidelines for Selecting Bias-Free Textbooks and Story Books*. New York: Council on Interracial Books for Children, 1980.

Hirschfelder, A.B. *American Indian Stereotypes in the World of Children: A Reader and Bibliography*. Metuchen, N.J.: Scarecrow Press, 1982.

Seale, D. "Bibliographies About Native Americans—A Mixed Blessing." *Bulletin of the Council on Interracial Books for Children* 12, no. 3 (1981): 11-15.

Stensland, A.L. *Literature by and about the American Indian*. Urbana, Ill.: National Council of Teachers of English, 1979.

TEN QUICK WAYS TO ANALYZE CHILDREN'S BOOKS FOR SEXISM AND RACISM

1. **Check the Illustrations.**

   Look for stereotypes.

   Look for tokenism. Who's doing what (active, leadership roles *vs.* passive, subservient roles)?

2. **Check the Story Line.**

   Standard for success (via "white" behavior or extraordinary abilities).

   Resolution of problems (are minorities the "problem" or are problems solved only by Anglos?).

   Role of women.

3. **Look at the Lifestyles**.

   Check for inaccuracies, inappropriate or oversimplified depictions of Indian cultures.

4. **Consider the Relationships Between People.**

   Who has power, exhibits leadership, and solves problems and how are families depicted?

5. **Note the Heroes.**

   Whose interests is a particular hero serving?

6. **Consider the Effects on a Child's Self-Image.**

7. **Consider the Author's or Illustrators Background.**

   Assess qualifications to write about the topic.

8. **Examine the Author's Perspective.**

   Look for a particular ethnocentric perspective.

9. **Watch for Loaded Words.**

   Look for words with offensive overtones.

10. **Look at the Copyright Date.**

    Older books are often more laden with racism than those published more recently.

(Council on Interracial Books for Children 1980)

APPENDICES

APPENDIX A

INDIAN AWARENESS INVENTORY

DIRECTIONS: Circle the letter that represents what you know to be true (**T**) or false (**F**). If you are unsure of the answer, circle unsure (**U**). This is a personal inventory developed to help you determine your knowledge about Native Americans. Do not try to guess.

	TRUE	FALSE	UNSURE
1. Since many Indian people live close to nature, they tend to be healthier than non-Indians.	T	F	U
2. Most Indians are proud of being Indian.	T	F	U
3. Most Indian men do not need to shave.	T	F	U
4. Most Indians receive free hospitalization.	T	F	U
5. Because of past treaties, Indian people do not have to register for the Armed Forces.	T	F	U
6. Indian people have the highest suicide rate of any group in the country.	T	F	U
7. Most Indian people do not pay taxes.	T	F	U
8. On the majority of reservations, Indian people need permission to leave.	T	F	U
9. Many Indian men still refer to their wives as squaws.	T	F	U
10. The majority of all Indian families carry water one mile or more to their homes.	T	F	U
11. Indian tribes are culturally deprived in some parts of the country.	T	F	U
12. Indians originated the practice of scalping their enemies.	T	F	U
13. Most Indian children attend Bureau of Indian Affairs schools.	T	F	U
14. Most Indians are carefree and happy people.	T	F	U
15. Because of religious beliefs, many Indians do not carry insurance.	T	F	U
16. Indians use the phrase "low man on the totem pole" to refer to a person in a group who has the lowest status.	T	F	U
17. Most Indians have high cheekbones.	T	F	U
18. Some Indians are still Indian givers.	T	F	U
19. In some states, Indian people are not to vote in elections.	T	F	U
20. Twenty percent of Indian families have no houses of their own.	T	F	U

21. Because of conflicting values, Indian people tend to have a high rate of failure in business.	T	F	U
22. Indians are usually good hunters.	T	F	U
23. The academic achievement level of most Indian children is below that of white children.	T	F	U
24. Because of their sense of direction, Indian people who come to the city can find their way around.	T	F	U
25. Indian people tend to be good farmers because of their reverence for the land.	T	F	U
26. In the last 75 years, Indians have lost over 40 percent of their land.	T	F	U
27. Indian athletes tend to be long-distance runners rather than sprinters.	T	F	U
28. Most tribes still have chiefs.	T	F	U
29. A person who is 1/5 Indian is called a "half-breed."	T	F	U
30. Indians tend to die younger than non-Indians.	T	F	U
31. An Indian man received a war bonnet when he became a chief.	T	F	U
32. The majority of Indian youth drop out of school by the tenth grade.	T	F	U
33. Because of genetic factors, many Indian people are alcoholics.	T	F	U
34. Some Indians get funds from the United States government for living on a reservation.	T	F	U
35. Fewer than 5 percent of Indian children have an Indian teacher.	T	F	U
36. Many Indian men make good auto mechanics because of their experience with arts and handicrafts.	T	F	U
37. Indians comprise less that 1 percent of the total population of the United States	T	F	U
38. President Nixon stated publicly that Native Americans are the most deprived and isolated group in our nation.	T	F	U
39. The average income of Indian Americans is $1500 a year.	T	F	U
40. There are laws that prohibit Indian people from drinking alcoholic beverages.	T	F	U

INSTRUMENT DEVELOPED BY: John Fletcher (Blackfoot), Church Ross (Lakota), and Gary Kush (non-Indian).

SCORING KEY AND ITEM EXPLANATION

1. FALSE. Just because one lives close to the land does not necessarily mean that one is healthy. Indians, for example, have the highest rate of tuberculosis of any ethnic group in the United States.

2. TRUE.

3. FALSE. One of the stereotypes of Indian people is that they do not need to shave. There are many stories of Indians in the past who pulled out their whiskers. Although some Indian men may still practice this procedure, the majority of them shave.

4. FALSE. By treaty rights, Indians do receive hospitalization because Indian people gave up many things, including land. They have *paid* for the hospitalization.

5. FALSE. Because Indians are citizens of the United States, they are subject to the same regulations regarding the Armed Forces as are other citizens.

6. TRUE.

7. FALSE. On some reservations, Indian people do not have to pay property tax, but they usually pay sales and income taxes, as others do.

8. FALSE. Some treaties state that Indian people need permission to leave, but these treaties are seldom enforced today. People can come and go from the reservation as they wish.

9. FALSE. Although one might find some Indian men referring to their wives as squaws, the majority of Indian women today dislike this term.

10. TRUE.

11. FALSE. The answer to this question depends on what one understands by the term "culturally deprived." Indians certainly are not deprived of *a* culture. The question is, deprived of whose culture? If one means deprived of the Anglo-American culture, then it is true that some Indian people are culturally deprived.

12. FALSE. Indians probably learned the practice of scalping from whites.

13. FALSE. The majority of Indian children attend public schools (approximately 392,000 [1986] in public schools and only 38,000 [1987-1988] in B.I.A. schools).

14. FALSE. One cannot make a generalization like this about all people.

15. FALSE. There are no known Indian religious beliefs that categorically prevent someone from having insurance.

16. FALSE. In the non-Indian community, the term "low man on the totem pole" ususally refers to persons with the lowest status in a group. Some of the tribes in the Northwest, such as the Makahs, believe that the clan person of the greatest importance should be the first one up from the bottom of the totem pole. Therefore, to be the low man on the totem pole is to be a person of great importance.

17. FALSE. This is a stereotype similar to the stereotype of identifying certain racial or ethnic groups by distinctive facial features or other physical characteristics.

18. TRUE. This is a tricky question because it depends on what one means by the phrase, "Indian giver." An Indian giveaway is an event still practiced widely today in which a person gives away something of great importance to someone. This is done to show affection, but it is also a practice of an economic system in which people continually share with each other those things which are needed. Therefore, a person might give away a rifle to someone else and receive it back several years later. When the United States government was making treaties, they would often negotiate with a tribal person who did not have the authority to make that treaty. When another member of the tribe asked for this treaty back, the government representative, out of his ignorance of tribal government, would say that the Indian was an "Indian giver."

19. FALSE.

20. TRUE.

21. FALSE. Not necessarily so; for example, recent statistics published by the Indian-controlled Urban Indian Development Association reported that the success rate for the 100+ Indian controlled businesses in the Los Angeles area was more than 96 percent.

22. FALSE. This statement is false because it is an absolute. Some Indians are good hunters, and some are not. One learns how to be a hunter. It is not a matter or race.

23. TRUE.

24. FALSE. A sense of direction is not hereditary nor a matter of race. One learns directions. Indians get just as confused in a new city as non-Indians.

25. FALSE. Some Indians are good farmers, and others are not. Reverence for the land does not make one a good farmer. Good farming practices require education and experience.

26. TRUE.

27. FALSE. It is a stereotype that Indian athletes tend to be cross-country runners rather than sprinters.

28. FALSE. Most tribes today have tribal chairpersons, not chiefs.

29. FALSE. How could a person be one-fifth of anything? A child born of a white parent and an Indian parent is a half-breed.

30. TRUE. On the average, Indian people die at the age of 44 years as compared to 66 for non-Indians. In a recent unconfirmed study, however, the average Indian age at death was 64 years.

31. FALSE. A war bonnet was earned, not given like a crown to a king.

32. TRUE.

33. FALSE. There is a popular theory that Indian people have a genetic disposition for alcoholism, but this has never been proven.

34. FALSE. This is one of the most common stereotypes of Indians. They *do not* receive a check from the federal government.

35. TRUE.

36. FALSE. Just because one knows how to do beadwork does not mean that one knows how to change sparkplugs. Throughout history Indian people have been considered to be "good with their hands." The stereotype is contrary to the experience of the early missionaries who, in many letters, stated that they had a difficult time teaching Indian people how to "work with their hands."

37. TRUE. There are approximately 1,500,000 (1980 Census) Indian people in the United States and they are a fast-growing minority group. The stereotype is that Indian people are a "vanishing race"; but this is contrary to the facts.

38. TRUE. President Nixon made this statement in a speech to the nation in 1970.

39. TRUE.

40. FALSE. In some "dry" states, Indians, as other people, are prohibited from drinking; but no federal, state, or local laws, other than *tribal* laws, specifically prohibit Indians from drinking.

APPENDIX B

NATIVE AMERICANS: HISTORICAL PERSPECTIVE*

IMPORTANT EVENTS IN NATIVE AMERICAN-EUROPEAN RELATIONSHIPS

1513   Juan Ponce de Leon landed on the Florida peninsula while en route from Puerto Rico. The relationship between Europeans and North American Indians began.

1565   The Spaniards established the St. Augustine colony in Florida, the first settlement organized by Europeans in present-day United States.

1637   Connecticut colonists murdered more than 500 Native Americans when the Pequot tribe tried to stop the colonists from invading their territory. This massacre is known as the Pequot War.

1675-1676 King Philip, a Wampanoag chief, led a coalition of Indian troops that nearly defeated the English colonists. The colonists eventually defeated his forces and dismembered his body.

1680   The Pueblos rebelled against the Spaniards and drove them from Pueblo territory. Many Spaniards were killed during the uprising.

1754-1763 The French and Indian War, one of a series of wars in which the French and the British struggled for control of the eastern part of North America. Each nation vied for Indian support.

U.S.-NATIVE AMERICAN RELATIONSHIPS

1794   A group of Indians suffered a crushing defeat at Fallen Timbers in Ohio on August 20. In 1795, they were forced to sign a treaty that ceded large segments of their lands in the Northwest Territory to whites.

1812   The War of 1812, between the United States and Britain, caused deep factions among the Indian tribes because of their different allegiances. The Indian allies of the British were severely punished by the United States when the war ended.

1824   The Bureau of Indian Affairs (B.I.A.) established in the War Department.

1830   U.S. Congress passed the Indian Removal Act that authorized the removal of Indians from the east to west of the Mississippi and stated conditions under which removal could be legally undertaken.

---

* Dates in **boldface** are watershed events.

1831   U.S. Supreme Court recognized Indian tribes as "domestic dependent nations" within the United States. In an 1832 decision, the Court declared that such nations had a right to self-government.

1838-1839 Cherokee forcefully removed from Georgia to Indian Territory in present-day Oklahoma. Their poignant journey westward is recalled as the "Trail of Tears."

1864   Colorado militia killed nearly 300 Cheyennes in a surprise attack at Sand Creek after the Cheyenne leaders had negotiated an armistice. This incident is known as the Sand Creek Massacre.

1864   Navajos reject U.S. control during the Mexican War and are forced to walk 800 miles to Fort Sumner, New Mexico. Many Navajos died and the plan to force them to be farmers failed. They were allowed to walk back to their homeland. This is known as the Long Walk.

1871   U.S. Congress act prohibits making further treaties with Native tribes.

1876   Sioux tribes, under the leadership of Sitting Bull, wiped out Custer's Seventh Cavalry at Little Big Horn—one of the last victories for Native tribes.

1885   Helen Hunt Jackson's *A Century of Dishonor* published—the first influential book to dramatize the poignant plight of Indian people in the United States.

1886   The brave Apache warrior, Geronimo, surrendered to American forces in September 1886. His surrender marked the defeat of the Southwest tribes.

1887   U.S. Congress passed the General Allotment or Dawes Act designed to terminate partially the Indians' special relationship with the United States government. It proved to be disastrous for Native Americans.

1890   Three hundred Sioux killed in a massacre at Wounded Knee Creek in South Dakota.

1924   The Snyder Act made Native Americans citizens of the United States.

1928   The Meriam Survey recommended major changes in federal policy related to Indian affairs; many of its recommendations were implemented in subsequent years.

1934   The Wheeler-Howard Act made it possible for

In beauty it is done

in harmony it is written

in beauty and harmony it shall so be finished.

changing woman said it so.

Karen Harvey
Lisa Harjo
Jane Jackson

COLOPHON

This bu[...]ith
Microso[...]nto
Aldus Pa[...]ing
original [...]on
paper, s[...]ith
Adobe S[...]m-
ported i[...]ra-
Studio. [...]s.

Text and[...]are
set in H[...]

Final layo[...]rn-
loaded to[...]